The Practitioner's Guide to

PRODUCT MANAGEMENT

Also from General Assembly

The Practitioner's Guide to Web Development

The Practitioner's Guide to User Experience Design

GENERAL
ASSEMBLY

The Practitioner's Guide to

PRODUCT MANAGEMENT

—

Jock Busuttil

GRAND CENTRAL
PUBLISHING

NEW YORK   BOSTON

Grand Central Publishing
Hachette Book Group
1290 Avenue of the Americas
New York, NY 10104

www.HachetteBookGroup.com

Printed in the United States of America

RRD-C

First Edition: January 2015

10 9 8 7 6 5 4 3 2 1

Grand Central Publishing is a division of Hachette Book Group, Inc. The Grand Central Publishing name and logo is a trademark of Hachette Book Group, Inc.

The Hachette Speakers Bureau provides a wide range of authors for speaking events. To find out more, go to www.hachettespeakersbureau.com or call (866) 376-6591.

The publisher is not responsible for websites (or their content) that are not owned by the publisher.

Library of Congress Cataloging-in-Publication Data

Busuttil, Jock.
  The practitioner's guide to product management / Jock Busuttil. — First edition.
      pages cm
  Includes bibliographical references and index.
    ISBN 978-1-4555-4856-9 (hardback) — ISBN 978-1-4555-4855-2 (ebook)
1. Product management.   I. Title.
    HF5415.15.B78 2015
    658.5—dc23
                                                                2014036044

ISBNs: 978-1-4555-4856-9 (hc) and 978-1-4555-8814-5 (int'l pb)

For Jo

CONTENTS

FOREWORD   ix
   by Jake Schwartz, CEO, General Assembly

INTRODUCTION   1

CHAPTER 1
Balancing the Three Rings   5

CHAPTER 2
Knowing the Customers Better Than
   They Know Themselves   29

CHAPTER 3
You're Actually Managing People, Not Products   68

CHAPTER 4
The Fine Line Between Success and Failure   103

CHAPTER 5
Tender Loving Care of Time   139

CONCLUSION   163

ACKNOWLEDGMENTS   177

FURTHER READING   179

NOTES 181

INDEX 191

ABOUT THE AUTHOR 197

FOREWORD

Product management is arguably the most sought after position in tech. Every week I meet recent college graduates who want to know how to get into the field. What used to be viewed as something of a workhorse position—the "business" person on a software team—has blossomed into a highly prized role consisting of an alchemy of art and science. Expert PMs are true rock stars in their companies, blending a wide range of skills in pursuit of product perfection. When done well, product management is a great and inspiring thing to behold—a product team all marching in the same direction, toward building an experience or feature that serves the customer *even better*.

But what makes a good product manager? That's one of the great mysteries any organization seeking to truly delight customers must solve. Those who learn the essential skills can play an exciting and vital role in a company's success, whether in a small startup or a large, established firm. But what are those skills? And how do people get into product management?

Many hard skills are involved: communication, project management, analytics, and technical understanding. But a whole host of intangibles are also key: a certain kind of magic that comes primarily from experience. This book shares not only the hard skills but also some of the magic as well, and it is full of stories of the good, the bad, and the ugly of product development and launches. For example:

Why did the Segway fail to change the world? Why did those who love Fritos want nothing to do with Frito Lay Lemonade? How did Apple, the company that has honed product launches to a science, go off script in launching Apple Maps? This book reveals the ways in which product managers come to understand the market, and how they can keep teams working in harmony.

Our vision at General Assembly is to build a global community of individuals empowered to pursue work they love by offering a wide range of courses that share the practical insights that make the difference in a successful tech career. Since 2010, we have grown from one small space in New York City to nine campuses on four different continents offering courses ranging from twelve-week intensives to two-day introductions and two-hour workshops. Our community has grown to hundreds of thousands of students and practitioners, and, through this book, our community now includes you. As with the other books in the General Assembly series, we've sought to bring to you the essential, hands-on wisdom that is the hallmark of our courses. Our goal is to equip you with the perspective you need to become a product rock star, whether you're a beginner or an experienced product manager looking for ways to improve.

By reading this book, you are taking a vital and important step in pursuing a career you love, and we hope it will be a great help to you on that journey.

—Jake Schwartz
CEO, General Assembly

INTRODUCTION

When inventor Ross F. Housholder filed his patent[1] in 1979 for "forming a three-dimensional article in layers"—the process that would become 3-D printing—I doubt he envisaged his creation becoming as affordable and widely used as it has. Today, 3-D printers create everything from replacement human organs to rocket parts, food, and even self-replicating printers.[2] We have the privilege and good fortune to be living in a golden age of information and technology in which we can access the collective knowledge of the human race instantly, carry supercomputers in our pockets, and see today's greatest innovations become old news overnight. Through technology we have the means to enrich our work and leisure time in ways people even just a few years ago could only have dreamed about. It is easier, cheaper, and quicker than ever to create technology products in both software and hardware, and the pace of innovation is still accelerating. Standing in the eye of this maelstrom are product managers.

Product managers are there to marshal the chaos, to calmly remind everyone caught up in the technological gold rush that all this headlong product innovation can't exist just for its own sake; it has to have a purpose: to enrich the lives of the people who use the technology. Product management is one of those professions people tend to end up in more by luck than by design and then discover it's right for them. The role has never been more necessary or in demand for both technology startups and more established companies, and this is an exciting time to be a product manager.

This book is about the art, science, and skill of product management.

The world doesn't need yet another textbook introducing a methodology or framework on the subject, so I haven't written one. In fact, much of what you'll read in the chapters that follow will provide you with helpful examples of what *not* to do. I will give you the inside track on avoiding all the product management pitfalls I've stumbled into over the years.

I've collected some of the most intriguing stories I could find to illustrate to you what product management is *really* all about, and to tell you from my own personal experience not only how to be successful at it, but how to *enjoy* it. I'll tell you how the role came into being, how it's continuing to evolve, and why it's such good news that there's no prescribed route to becoming a product manager. While I'm at it, I'll show you how to determine value with a half-empty bottle of water and how Maslow made me a safer motorcyclist.

This book is also about products, so we'll delve into examples of the good, the bad, and the ill-advised to learn why they succeeded or failed. Navigating the fine line between product success and product failure is one of the trickiest parts of the job, and I'll introduce the product manager's set of navigational tools, including the nine most effective ways you can increase your product's chances of success. We'll look at how a Japanese professor devised a way to predict customer delight, the story of the hundred-million-dollar assumption, how a riddle from ancient Greece can bring your product greater success, and how woodworkers and the Large Hadron Collider at CERN can help you determine your target market. I'll uncover how focus groups nearly caused the Reebok Pump to be stillborn and how difficult it can be to avoid testing bias in Rwanda. I'll also clear away some common misunderstandings about Lean Startup theory and show you how Apple and Google create their minimum viable products (MVPs) the right way.

The launch of a product is an art form all its own, and we'll take a look at the many lessons leading brands have learned the hard way in launches, and how even Apple, the master of the craft, could orchestrate a stunning failure. I'll show you why a humble roadmap is the best way to help a team stay on course, and we'll look at why you sometimes need to fail, why you should look forward to a good crisis, and why Netflix deliberately sabotages its own systems from time to time.

What kinds of people will you be working with? We'll take a look at the full team, and I'll draw on the many lessons I've learned the hard way to help you survive unscathed and even enjoy the experience. I'll share with you how situational leadership made me a better manager, why emails are as addictive as slot machines, and why sometimes you just have to say no to people.

Because there are so many people and parts of the process to keep track of, managing time may be the most foundational skill of a good product manager. I'll share the methods I've found most helpful, revealing why there's no point in trying to multitask; why so many of us, including myself, have a natural tendency to procrastinate and how to overcome that; and how an ancient paradox can help you manage complex tasks more easily. Thank you for accompanying me on this journey. May it be as enjoyable for you to read as it has been for me to write.

Chapter 1

BALANCING THE THREE RINGS

—

Plummeting tail-first into cloud cover (where I shouldn't have been) at the controls of a Bulldog T1 trainer aircraft, a few thousand feet above Royal Air Force Mildenhall's military air traffic zone (where I *definitely* shouldn't have been), I realized three things:

1. I'd failed miserably to execute a relatively straightforward maneuver called a stall turn.
2. I had to learn to prioritize the task at hand rather than allow my inner monologue to distract me.
3. I probably wasn't cut out to be a pilot in the RAF.

While I'd love to proclaim, "And that's when I knew I was born to be a product manager," my route into the profession was more circuitous, as it is for almost all product managers. I had been planning to join the RAF when I finished my undergraduate studies, but that flawed stall turn told me I would have to switch to plan B. (Not a bad lesson for a future product manager, about which more later.) I'd never even heard of the role of product manager when I graduated, though.

Even today relatively few people outside the world of technology have heard of the job. When I'm at a party and someone inevitably asks, "So, what do you do for a living?" I always have to explain that product management is different from *project* management. (At which point my companion often hurries away to the bar. Now I sometimes just tell people I train dolphins.)

There's a good reason the job isn't better understood. Although it originated in the world of consumer products, product management is now mainly associated with the high-tech sphere and is rapidly evolving to keep up with the pace of innovation. It's this breed of product management the book focuses on, though many of the fundamentals are the same and apply to the job as practiced in any sector.

WHAT *IS* PRODUCT MANAGEMENT?

One of the best descriptions of what a product manager does was crafted by Martin Eriksson, a product manager I've known and respected for a number of years who started the hugely successful ProductTank monthly meetup series in London.[1] Eriksson describes the product manager's role as it changes through the life cycle of a product. First, the job is not only to define the vision for the product, but to understand the product's market and target customers and then to work with the product team to add a dose of creativity to make the product more alluring. It's then about evangelizing the product vision and inspiring those making the product with that passion.

Switching from the creative to the analytical part of the brain, a product manager proceeds to plan how to actually execute that vision through product iterations, design, and roadmaps. Then, zooming in from the broad plan to the fine detail, there's the day-to-day problem-solving, working with the development, design, and other teams to remove the obstacles in the path of the product while keeping the overall plan on track, and working with the marketing and sales teams to plan and execute the launch. After launch, the job becomes gathering and poring over information about how people are eating, sleeping, and breathing the product in order to assess its success. Then you do it all over again.

As you can imagine, the job is somewhat like spinning plates;* it's a tricky balancing act to switch focus continually between the long and short term, the big picture and the fine detail. That's a large part of what makes the work so stimulating and why a successful product manager requires a diverse set of social, commercial, and technical skills, and above all else the ability to empathize and communicate with many different groups of people on their own terms.

THE THREE RINGS

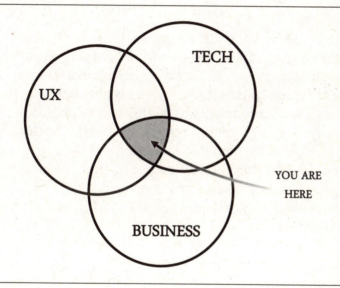

Product management Venn diagram courtesy of Martin Eriksson (http://www .martineriksson.com) and Mind the Product (http://www.mindtheproduct.com)

---

* Erich Brenn on *The Ed Sullivan Show* seems to capture what product management feels like: *The Ed Sullivan Show*, YouTube, last modified August 25, 2009, http://youtu.be/Zhoos1oY404.

The product manager is right there at the center of it all, negotiating the inevitable push and pull between the needs of the users (user experience, or UX), the demands of the business, and what happens to be possible (or not) with the available technology. The three-rings diagram that illustrates this concept was created by Martin Eriksson. He jokes that only a product manager would think of the job in terms of a Venn diagram, but I think the image is very helpful as a shorthand overview of the dynamics within a company as it creates, launches, and evolves a product—and as a reminder of the challenges that arise in the eye of the storm. Let's take a closer look at each ring of the diagram.

UX

People often interpret the UX ring purely as representing the user experience *team*, that is, the people within your organization responsible for the design of your products' interactions with users. Instead, I'd like you to think of this in the much broader sense of the *experience of your users*. More importantly, this ring encompasses not only your UX team but also your target market—specifically, the needs and problems faced by the intended users and buyers of your product, the context in which they operate, and the way they experience your company and product, not just the specifics of how features are designed to solve their problems. The UX ring represents the **outside world and its needs**.

Business

Whether your company is for-profit or not-for-profit, at a bare minimum it needs to sustain itself, and its ability to do so is dependent on the success of the products and services it offers. From the perspective of the business, a successful product is one that is used and valued by customers, and one that is profitable. A business also has other needs, such as maintaining its reputation with customers and its relationship with investors, as well as all the practicalities of operating on a day-to-day basis. The business ring represents the **needs and aspirations of your organization**.

Tech

The pace of technological change is rapid, so a product manager needs to keep on top of the advances being made and understand the strengths and weaknesses of the technologies that will play a part in the creation of the product. Opportunities can arise simply because a recent innovation renders a problem more easily or cheaply solved than before. Your development team (which some companies call *engineering*) plays a crucial part as your interface to these technologies and in realizing the product vision. The tech ring represents both the **technologies and technologists that shape your product**.

ACHIEVING BALANCE

I'd love to continue by telling you how wonderfully easy it is to sit at the center of the three rings in complete and masterful control, but I'd be lying through my teeth. Some days it can feel like you've roped yourself into the hub of a bizarre tug-of-war between the various groups of people you deal with—and they're all pulling you in different directions. But in the challenge lies the reward. We don't do this because it's easy—we do it because we can.

The good news is that there are only so many tensions that can crop up among the three rings; thereafter they're just variations on a theme. From time to time, senior management will throw wrenches into the works, development teams will head off track on science projects, marketing teams will ignore inconvenient facts that spoil their message, design teams will create beautiful but impractical mockups, sales teams will be concerned with their commission over all else, finance teams will keep you as far away as possible from their numbers, and legal teams will veto anything that has even a whiff of risk. We'll delve into the issues regarding managing and communicating with the team in chapter 3. Finding the right balance between the three rings is tricky. It's surprising how many companies delude themselves into thinking that they've achieved a balance between the needs of their market, their own business aspirations, and the available technology. Companies often go off course by almost completely ignoring their market, perhaps because they've become too enamored with their own technology or because their own corporate objectives have distracted them, or sometimes both. (We'll take a look at a few cautionary tales in the next chapter.) That's why more and more companies are beginning to realize that they need to restore balance to be successful. They have a significant, urgent, and valuable problem that's solved by hiring good product managers. (How supremely handy for those getting into the profession!)

Most people who know a little about product management think it's a new discipline, a technology role for the technology age. Actually, its roots go way back to the first half of the twentieth century, to a maverick at Procter & Gamble, purveyor of such global brand giants as Gillette, Duracell, and Pampers. P&G has always been an innovator. The company started out in 1837 as a humble soap and candle maker.[2] By the 1930s, it had diversified into cooking and household cleaning products, and when it pioneered product sponsorship of shows on network radio by sponsoring the *Ma Perkins* radio serial, what we know as the soap opera was born.

In 1931 a young and ambitious promotion manager named Neil McElroy, who had been put in charge of promoting the Camay soap brand, was frustrated that Camay always played second fiddle to P&G's leading brand, Ivory. In a famous memo to management, he argued for the creation of the role of "brand manager."[3] This person would take overall responsibility for the commercial success of a product, managing it holistically like a business in its own right, conducting field studies and collaborating with other departments within the company.

The role as it's now performed in the tech sector is in many ways fundamentally the same, but it has been tailored to tech needs and capabilities.

This is a great time to get into the profession because it's become a more dynamic role in recent years. When product management was first adopted by the tech sector, products were created using the Waterfall serial project development process. All the product requirements were defined up front, and then the product was built, tested (maybe), and launched (thrown haphazardly out the door). Midproject changes were almost impossible to make, and particularly nimble companies managed two or—gasp!—three releases a year. Over the last decade or so, innovations in technology have opened up new ways of working. With the strong influence of Silicon Valley leaders like Google, eBay, and Facebook, product management evolved into a more central role, and it's now undergoing another wave of change.

This new wave is driven by many factors: the explosion of web-based development tools; standardization of the use of particular programming languages, software frameworks, and platforms; and, most of all, data. Arguably product management always has been driven by data—McElroy advocated the use of field studies to gather data "to determine whether the plan has produced the expected results"[4]—but the key difference now is that data is so much more readily accessible, more easily analyzed in greater quantities, and often available in real time.

Organizations have begun using their new capabilities to apply rapid iteration methodologies derived from Lean Manufacturing[5] to product development. It has become easy to test whether a hypothetical change would improve a product by actually building multiple versions and running a randomized controlled experiment (also known as a split or A/B test) to see which one performs better with actual users. Imagine you're trying to improve the click-through rate for a particular button on a web page and you believe that making the button more prominent will achieve this. To test this hypothesis, you would show different pages with variations of the button, including the original version (or *control*), to visitors at random, comparing the results to see which version has the best click-through rate. Such real-time data analytics allow companies to rapidly improve products, sometimes creating many iterations in a single day.

Part of a class I teach on product management involves the students practicing their quick-draw wireframing skills by sketching a well-known website on the whiteboard for the rest of the class to guess, like a geekier version of Pictionary. One of the websites I ask students to draw is Facebook. The reaction is invariably the same: first the student smiles with recognition, thinking it easy to draw. He thinks about it a little more. A look of mild confusion replaces the smile as the student realizes he can only remember what it looked like a few years ago, usually before the introduction of the timeline. Facebook's founder, Mark Zuckerberg, described one aspect of his company's philosophy as: "Move fast and break things."[6] Instead of running extensive focus groups on every new feature to gauge its users' reaction, Facebook just sends the features live,[7] making changes only when the users' howls of annoyance become loud enough, as was the case with Beacon, an ill-advised privacy land-grab.[8] But analyzing data is just one of a blend of techniques Facebook uses, as Nate Bolt, head of design research at the company, describes:

> It's common for studies to have three or four redundant data gathering methods. Some of those data gathering methods will be qualitative and some will be quantitative. We have a pretty badass analytics team that's gonna give us trends and insights and show us things happening on the mobile builds that we wouldn't get out of qualitative testing. And then a lot of times, we'll go investigate with the qualitative stuff.[9]

This is one way in which the role of the product manager is so important: in balancing the hard and soft sides—or left-brain versus right-brain factors—in developing and launching products. Data analytics can be a siren call luring a company away from listening *in a more qualitative way* to its market, neglecting human measures such as satisfaction and enjoyment. As Aaron Levenstein, professor emeritus of Baruch College, delightfully put it, "Statistics are like bikinis. What they reveal is suggestive, but what they conceal is vital."

Which is why the right-brain interpretive and creative skills are still so important to the job. Replacing all direct market contact with pure data analytics just doesn't present the full picture. Despite having around one billion users worldwide[10] on whom to run multivariate tests,[11] even Facebook cannot rely on data analytics alone—it still needs to engage with and listen to its market.

OWNERSHIP AND VISION

A product manager's role is to own and be ultimately responsible for one or more product lines. And that means really *own*. To say that the buck stops with the product manager is an understatement. A true product manager will go and *find* the buck that's buried on someone's desk. But to be effectual, this ownership must come with the authority to make the decisions needed to steer the product to success. With their combination of extensive market understanding, intuition, and creativity, product managers are the people who can see a new opportunity emerging; visualize the product needed to take advantage of that opportunity; then enthuse, corral, and provide the necessary detail to the various specialists they work with in order to bring the product to life. Sometimes that new opportunity arises unexpectedly from the development of another product, as the scientists at Pfizer found with their new drug, sildenafil citrate. Although it was originally designed to lower blood pressure and treat angina, early clinical trials showed that the intended improvement in blood flow caused by sildenafil also happened to cause male erections. The drug is now better known as Viagra. But more often the product manager must recognize that the market has moved on,[12] so the product in turn must change or be killed off.

A product manager's role is essentially about providing three things: context, perspective, and vision. The context is a portrait of the real people in the market who have a particular problem or need, and describes the environment in which they experience it. That might be when they're out walking their dog, working at their office, or driving in their car. Perspective provides an honest appraisal of how effectively the organization and its product are going about solving those problems. Possibly most important, vision is used to motivate and align everyone involved in creating a product by describing the product's potential.

Without strong product management, the vision can often be corrupted by organizations for a few common reasons.

They've Stopped Empathizing

People at a company that's focused on maximizing its revenues, profits, and share price to the exclusion of all else have probably ceased to care about their customers. They've become inwardly focused, forgotten about the outside world, and are more concerned with solving their own internal, corporate problems rather than those of their target market.

They've Forgotten the Real-World Benefits of Their Products

If a company's forgotten how to empathize with its customers, it's probably also in the dark about the *real-world* benefits its product brings to people's lives. Like how Jeff doesn't tear his hair out every time he uses the accounting system. Or how Clarissa, who's lost all her wedding photos because of a broken hard drive, discovers they've been automatically backed up to the cloud without her realizing it.

They've Stopped Dreaming

People don't *dream* of being given coupons in the supermarket, or finding a convenient parking space, or washing the dishes; they dream of going into space, or getting a job as chief taster in a chocolate factory, or discovering a new exotic particle. A product vision should be dreamlike in the sense that it has to be worthy of chasing so that people can anticipate their future sense of achievement and use that feeling as motivation to fight for it. It has to matter.[13] Dharmesh Raithatha, once a senior product manager at Mind Candy, the company responsible for Moshi Monsters, described how Mind Candy repeatedly evolved its product vision to ensure it was always just out of reach.[14] Your product vision must be a shining goal, a guiding star that everyone in the organization can visualize, so they become passionate about it and align themselves with it.

Organizations that create a mundane vision—"We want to be the dominant player in the *blah blah blah* market"—fail to motivate their workforces. With an uninspiring vision, dysfunction will seep in as self-motivated departments, teams, and individuals reject the vision and create their own guiding star to follow instead. In organizations without strong product management it is much harder to achieve alignment to a common goal because there is no single and consistent voice evangelizing the product vision, reminding everyone that they come to work each day to make the lives of people like Jeff and Clarissa just a little bit better.

A PROFESSION IN FLUX

Though the fundamental purpose of product management is widely agreed upon, you will inevitably encounter several competing but intersecting schools of thought on the role and its responsibilities. One view is that a product manager should be involved only in the identification of market opportunities (the "problem space") and in no way with addressing that opportunity (the "solution space"); another view holds that the product manager must be responsible for defining both the problem and solution spaces. Google and other technology-led Silicon Valley giants will only accept candidates for the role of product manager if they have a computer science degree; other companies value and seek breadth of experience, irrespective of what the candidate happened to major in. These competing views and methodologies are frequent topics of heated debate within the product management community.[15] To a newcomer, however, they must be positively perplexing and perhaps a little off-putting—how on earth are you meant to understand your role if the practitioners themselves don't agree on what's involved? So to keep things simple, the true crux of the job, no matter how it's defined and what responsibilities you're given, is to **focus on the users**. They're the ones with the problem you're trying to solve. Everything else is secondary.

What I would *not* recommend, as you learn about product management, is to adhere slavishly to the precepts and principles of any one particular framework or methodology. Use the Japanese principle of *kaizen*—continual improvement—and apply it to both your products and yourself.[16] Try techniques out, keep what works, discard what doesn't. Product management frameworks are a dime a dozen, and every company wants you to buy into its mindset and ecosystem of blogs, training, and books. The constant pressure on product managers to align themselves into factions citing the Silicon Valley, Lean, Google, or another approach as the One True Path is divisive nonsense. I've yet to encounter an organization that does product management in precisely the same way as another. In fact, I expect (and encourage) companies to tailor product management to suit their market, products, maturity, and culture. What won't vary from place to place is that you should always be focused on the needs of your users and that you'll need to collaborate with the specialists across all the departments in your company to bring your product vision to life.

If you're working in a startup as a product manager, the job will be even more variable. You'll be expected to roll up your sleeves and do a much broader variety of jobs. When I worked at a startup called Zeus Technology, I fulfilled roles ranging from trainer to IT manager to product marketer, all at the same time.

With the burgeoning demand, you'd think there would be more university courses, and even degrees, in the field. A handful of universities and business schools are in fact now offering degrees specifically in product management,[17] and a good MBA course will teach you many of the skills needed to become a product manager, though in my view these programs can be too biased toward business theory rather than a more practical approach balanced across the three rings. A plethora of professional organizations worldwide offer product management training and certification. However, not all courses are equal, and without a standard benchmark for qualification, you have to be extra diligent when assessing the merits of the course you're considering. Also, the fact is that product management is really a learning-by-doing job. So two tips: first, try to be taught by active product managers rather than those who gave up client work years ago; and second, choose instructors who have experience in the kinds of companies in which you would like to work.

I don't think the dearth of undergraduate or postgraduate courses in the theory of product management is necessarily a hindrance to those on their journey into the field. Having a range of educational, social, and work experience, whether in or outside of technology, will give you the benefit of a broader perspective as well as diverse creative and technical skills such as communication, design, organization, and structured and lateral thinking. All these will better equip you to swap hats with ease between the different roles required of product managers.

The product people I've had the pleasure of meeting over the years have made their way into product management from wildly diverse backgrounds. Alison started out in UX but was frustrated by "crappy product decisions" by "the business" and set out to see if she could do better as a product manager, while simultaneously mounting a personal crusade against people who use terms like "the business." A senior software engineer called Pritesh told me he felt there was too great a divide between him and the users. He wanted to spend more time understanding how people were actually using his product and start building products that solved problems for real people. It was at this point that he discovered the role of product manager. Tom, with whom I worked for many years, started a company straight out of college, sold it, then discovered that being a product manager was closest to what he'd enjoyed doing as an entrepreneur, albeit with a more predictable salary. Then there are others who turned up to work one day to find that their job title had changed without warning to product manager and were just expected to figure it out themselves. So don't be dissuaded from starting your journey into the profession because you feel you don't have the right background; we all have experience that can be highly valuable. Your product experience is, after all, the product of your experiences. There's no such thing as a conventional route into product management—take my own story as a case in point.

FROM PLANES TO PRODUCTS

Ever since reading Roald Dahl's *Going Solo* when I was young, I had dreamed of becoming a Royal Air Force pilot, so that flawed stall turn over the English countryside was a real moment of truth for me.

The mighty Scottish Aviation Bulldog (Courtesy of Geoff Collins)

Failing to execute the turn correctly before running out of forward momentum is a Bad Thing". Going backward at speed in an airplane tends to cause bits to tear off. The danger didn't seem to bother my flying instructor, a former frontline RAF station commander, in the slightest. He had his hands away from the stick because I was "in control." With the wind whistling past in the wrong direction and our reverse speed mounting, he gave an almost imperceptible sigh of resignation and calmly advised me to simply brace the controls firmly and let the nose-heavy aircraft sort itself out.

Not all my training flights were quite so inept, but it was clear to me that I wasn't learning at a pace quick enough for the RAF's intensive, rapid-fire training. With that career off the table, I focused on my undergraduate studies in my wonderfully practical major, classics. The study of the ancient world is a broad subject, covering everything from the linguistics of Ancient Greek and Latin to anthropology, architecture, poetry, and philosophy. It teaches you how to think and how to learn, but it's not the most obviously vocational of subjects, and I didn't think I would cut it as an academic. Thankfully, I'd become progressively more involved with computing, partly by accident. What started out as helping the student union tweak its website turned into managing its book publishing systems and network.

I also helped set up and run a free web hosting and email service that's still prospering today.[18] This had the side effect of introducing me to the community of computer scientists. Now I don't want to give you the impression that I'd actually learned much real coding, and at the university's annual job fair, I was laughed off the stands by most of the recruiting software firms as soon as I mentioned I was studying classics. For them it was computer science or nothing. A friend fortunately referred me to a company named (fittingly, for a classics major) Zeus Technology.[19] It was a startup based in Cambridge, England, famed at the time for producing the "world's fastest web server"[20] and, for a while, powering eBay's global search engine.[21] The company was willing to take a chance on me, and so in August 2000, I began my first full-time job, on the Zeus technical support desk.

On day one, my manager deposited three hefty tomes on MySQL, Perl, and PHP on my desk and suggested I start reading, as I'd need to understand them to help resolve customers' support queries by the following week. I now understand why: the product itself (Zeus Web Server) was rock-solid stable. We had customers who had installed it years before and had never had to restart it, let alone experienced any problems. Consequently a large proportion of customer questions had nothing to do with the product itself but rather dealt with the other software apps they ran with it. So partly because we had time to and partly because we on the support desk enjoyed it, we solved pretty much any problem our customers sent us. I distinctly remember spending hours talking a customer through a full system install, from bare metal upward. I found that solving customers' problems was addictive.

Over the course of several years at Zeus, I cycled through a variety of technical roles, including web development and IT support (I was the guy swearing under the desk with a network cable). The dotcom bubble burst and three-quarters of the company was laid off. The people who were left had to start wearing several hats—at one point I was simultaneously the IT department, technical presales consultant, webmaster,* customer trainer, internal systems developer, product marketer, and, briefly, receptionist. While I'd been working in technical presales, and in the absence of a marketing department, I'd found myself creating product brochures and website material for prospective clients. I enjoyed the writing and publishing, and it wasn't a massive leap from there to looking after "the message"—how we presented our company and products to our market.

There were two aspects of my job in product marketing that I particularly enjoyed: writing customer case studies and conducting win-loss interviews. Win-loss interviews involve calling up people who have either bought the product or decided not to in order to ask them

---

* There's a job role you don't see anymore. I always thought it should come with some kind of horned Viking helmet.

Boone County Public Library
Check Out Receipt

Date charged: July 11, 2019
11:40 AM
Item ID: 204091009954713
Title: The practitioner's
guide to product
management
Date due: August 1, 2019
11:59 PM

Date charged: July 11, 2019
11:40 AM
Item ID: 204091009141761
Title: Windows 8 simplified
Date due: August 1, 2019
11:59 PM

Total checkouts for session:
2
Total checkouts:2

Thank You
.
.
.
.
.
.
.
.
.

why.[22] Without exception, the conversations with the people who had chosen not to buy were far more enlightening. I started to learn where we'd gone wrong with our sales approach, marketing content, reseller management, pricing strategy, and product features. I began to get a feel for why we were missing out on opportunities and started to think about what we could do better next time. I took my suggestions to the head of development, who, in retrospect, was the de facto product manager, but I was "just" a product marketing manager—didn't I have enough work to be getting on with already? I wanted to influence product strategy but didn't know how I could. So I did some research and established that there was in fact a role that blended technical, commercial, and user-facing skills and looked after product strategy.

And that's when I knew I was born to be a product manager.

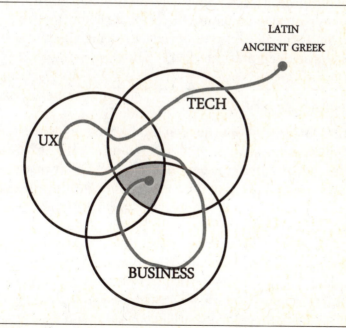

My own path to product management was by no means direct.

In your own journey toward becoming a product manager, you can think of the three rings again, this time as a map for making your transition into the field. Each ring represents a different continent of experience you need to visit. Your starting point on your route may be within one of the three continents, or in a completely different area of expertise even farther afield. To end up at the intersection in the middle, you need to have journeyed through all three continents at least once. You can do so by working your way through different roles, as I did; by taking classes in each area; or, ideally, by doing both. However, there is no prescribed path, no right or wrong way to become a product manager—and every product person's story is different.

So celebrate your degree in Chaucerian literature, marine biology, modern languages, or perhaps even computer science! Rejoice that you were the head of your school's debating society, played football at club level, or organized charity events each year. Brag about the fact that you recorded an album in your bedroom or spent a summer fixing the plumbing in convents—product management welcomes students graduating from the university of life.

WHAT QUALITIES MAKE FOR A GOOD PRODUCT MANAGER?

When you're looking for your dream product management role, many of the job descriptions you'll read will state that the recruiting company is looking for domain experience in a particular market or technology. If you happen to have this experience, that's a bonus, but if you don't, don't be discouraged! There are a few highly specialized exceptions, such as semiconductors, pharmaceuticals, and bioinformatics, but in general I don't believe it's necessary for a product manager to have previous experience with the markets, technologies, or products she'll be working with. However, it is vital that you can learn quickly. Each company you work for will use different technologies to build different products for different markets with different dynamics. The faster you're able to build up a decent working knowledge of each, the sooner you'll be able to take ownership of your products. As a rule of thumb you should be able to do this within a month of joining a new company. The ability and desire to learn and understand are, in my opinion, among the most fundamental attributes of a product manager.

Achieving a good blend of technical, commercial, and user experience skills is important, but I don't think there is—or should be—a fixed recipe for the cocktail that is a good product manager. I do, however, think there are certain traits that predispose people to be effective at product management. Before going any farther, don't feel you should treat this as a definitive list or worry that you don't exhibit some of these characteristics; I am still working hard to improve several of these myself. With that in mind, quality product managers:

» are sponges for quickly absorbing, understanding, and retaining information;
» are excellent listeners;
» are great communicators, mediators, and educators;
» can keep their heads when all about are losing theirs and blaming it on the product manager (with apologies to Kipling);
» can see both the bigger picture and the fine detail;
» are consummate problem solvers and fixers;
» are not afraid to roll up their sleeves and do something themselves if nobody else is bothering to;
» have a calming effect on others;
» always have a plan B;
» have an eye for spotting an opportunity, whether commercial or technical;
» are natural organizers;
» are capable of running a project successfully, but would not like being thought of as project managers;*

---

* The clue's in the name: a project manager's scope of responsibility is the good running of a project, often within the confines of product development only and with a specific timescale and set of objectives. The project by definition is short-lived. In contrast, a product manager's scope of responsibility is the good

- » will be able to pitch their product better than anyone else, but don't want to have to do sales' or marketing's job for them;
- » take negative criticism with good grace and continually seek to do better;
- » like being recognized for doing a good job, but rarely solicit praise for themselves;
- » recognize the efforts of others before their own;
- » treat a problem not as a setback, but as an opportunity to make things better;
- » have a natural curiosity and interest;
- » continually test their (and others') assumptions;
- » tend to excel in something completely unrelated to their job—whether as cooks, musicians, writers, or linguists;
- » hate feeling ineffective—take away their responsibilities, authority, or budget or stop listening to them and you'll soon find yourself with a product-manager-shaped gap in your organization.

If these traits resonate with you, if you feel many of them describe you and the way you like to work, then well done! You're in good shape for becoming an expert product manager.

LEARN THE BASICS BUT AVOID DOGMA

No matter what stage you are at in your journey to becoming a product manager—whether just thinking about getting into the profession or in the midst of taking classes, or maybe, as I did, having just plunged in from a different role—it's important to get a good grounding in the full range of what the job requires and how it works. Reading this book is a good start, and there is plenty of other great writing to follow up with. (I make some recommendations at the end of the book.)

---

running of a product, on a holistic and open-ended basis, with a set of objectives that evolve with the changing needs of the target market. A single product will have many projects (and project managers) throughout its life, but its product manager will ideally be more constant.

As I've said, taking at least a basic class is also highly recommended for gaining a solid foundation to build on. I certainly benefited a great deal from some brief formal training when I started out.

In my first product manager job, I was fortunate to find an employer that packed me off to a product boot camp soon after I joined the firm. Off I went to Boston, Massachusetts, to receive a week of training with Steve Johnson, then at Pragmatic Marketing. Reflecting back, I recall enjoying the focus on the user's needs and the repeated mantra, "Your opinions, though interesting, are irrelevant"—useful for reminding yourself that you, the product manager, are not the target market. I also remember feeling reassured that a great deal of product management boiled down to common sense and that what I'd been doing up to that point had not been too far off the mark despite working from first principles. After the course, I also appreciated having a framework to follow that corresponded with the way the company wanted us to manage the products and that gave me structured ways of thinking about a particular problem, allowing me to reframe it in a way that made it easier to solve. So I definitely recommend learning and following some kind of framework at the outset of your career as a product manager.

As I've mentioned, there are several product management courses and frameworks out there. Naturally, I highly recommend General Assembly's product management course as an introduction to many of the fundamental concepts (not least because I teach it). I personally happened to start out with Pragmatic Marketing, whose framework breaks down product management into distinct strategic and tactical activities. You could try Silicon Valley Product Group's recommended practices for the West Coast technology perspective and Sequent Learning Networks' courses for slightly more of an East Coast business bias. Blackblot in Europe has a very structured approach, which may be more helpful for more heavily regulated, process-driven companies, and Product Focus in the UK specializes in product management for telecoms and IT. There are, of course, many other training providers and frameworks out there, with varying levels of quality and relevance. Your mileage may vary.

Whichever framework you start with, whether it's one you've been taught or the process that's already in place at the company you join, it's important to keep in mind that *people* drive the *process*, not the other way around. Even if you start with a textbook implementation of a particular framework or set of best practices, it's inevitable and important that you tailor the process to suit the needs of your market, company, and product and continue to adapt, evolve, and improve it as you go along. It's unlikely you'll ever find yourself following one of these frameworks in lockstep, even if you're totally in charge of your process. This need for ongoing change simply reflects the fact that markets do not stand still. Product management had to evolve to respond to and capitalize on the opportunity presented by social media; online productivity tools are now much more widely available than in the past but can easily lead to a very fragmented, inconsistent, and confusing approach if every person on every project does similar tasks in completely different ways. To retain a modicum of control, you need to keep your process flexible enough to gain the benefits of consistent working practices while still allowing it freedom to evolve. However, if you find yourself in a situation where the people are serving the process instead of vice versa, there's a good chance that you're going about product management too dogmatically and missing a trick. Different situations, different products, different companies, and different markets will all call for different approaches. One size most certainly does not fit all.

Whichever path leads you into product management, I have one further piece of advice for you. Before accepting any product manager job offer, ask yourself the following questions:

» Does the product excite me?
» Does the market seem intriguing?
» Do I click with the people I'll be working with?

One "no" answer by itself is not a dealbreaker, but if you're able to say yes to only one of them, take this as a warning sign that the job may not be for you. Like any good product manager would, do your homework to reduce your uncertainties: Propose or accept any invitation to sit in with the team you'll be working with to get an idea of what the organization is like. Speak to former employees if you can find them on LinkedIn, but bear in mind their viewpoints may be embittered if they left on poor terms. Play with the company's products if you can get access to them, and note your first impressions and anything that surprises you; these observations are immensely valuable even if you're not the intended target user. It's also revealing to ask at the end of interviews why the product team does something in a particular way, not just to hear the actual answer but to see how defensively or openly the interviewer responds when someone challenges her approach.

Lastly, consider how the role will assist your professional development. Is it similar to something you've done before, perhaps reinforcing your natural bias toward one of the three rings? Or is it taking you a little out of your comfort zone and forcing you to gain more experience in areas where you're less skilled? It's perfectly fine to consolidate your existing skill set in a more senior, interesting role, just as it's fine to make a sideways move to build up your experience if that's what you need. What's important is that you're always striving toward a good balance between the three rings of product management.

POINTS TO REMEMBER

Balancing the Three Rings

» There's no such thing as a conventional route into product management. Learn by doing.
» A successful product manager requires a blend of social, commercial, and technical skills—above all else the ability to empathize and communicate with people on their own terms.

(continued)

» You own the product vision, and that vision must inspire, motivate, and be a guiding star to everyone in the organization.
» Data tells you what your users are doing, not why they're doing it. Don't be lured away from speaking and listening to your market directly.
» The practice of product management is still evolving, so focus on the fundamentals: understand your users and their problems, and solve those problems with a commercially viable product.

Chapter 2

KNOWING THE CUSTOMERS BETTER THAN THEY KNOW THEMSELVES

On the birthday of Apollo, the Greek sun god, devotees would make the arduous pilgrimage to his temple at Delphi, high on the slopes of Mount Parnassus above the Corinthian Gulf. The following inscription adorned the ancient stone walls that greeted them:

ΓΝΩΘΙ ΣΕΑΥΤΟΝ

"KNOW THYSELF" was an old maxim, ancient even to the visitors of the sixth century BCE. An oracle at the temple presaged the future through the interpreted ravings of the Pythia, the oracle's priestess and mortal mouthpiece. Kings, philosophers, and ordinary folk alike consulted the oracle for guidance, and in turn received the kind of ambiguous prophecy that might have made them think about asking for a refund of their votive offerings. Herodotus, a historian (and occasional teller of tall tales) living in the fifth century BCE, told of how King Croesus of Lydia (he of the famed wealth) had tested out various oracles to see which was the most accurate in prophesying and settled on the oracle at Delphi. Croesus later asked the oracle whether his army should check the advance of the strengthening Persian Empire into his country. He received the response, "If Croesus goes to war he will destroy a great empire." Satisfied, off he went to engage the Persians, only to be roundly defeated. The great empire he destroyed was, in the end, his own. One might wonder whether the dictum to know thyself was a warning about the dangers of failing to challenge our assumptions.

It would be wonderful if we knew ourselves sufficiently well not only to understand the assumptions we may be making, but to fully and clearly articulate our thoughts and needs. It would eliminate many misunderstandings we have with friends, family, and colleagues, and would obviate the reading between the lines and educated guessing that product managers must do so much of. One of the most important roles of the product manager is to understand people's compelling needs for products, but the trouble is that people rarely know their own minds well enough to distinguish between their fundamental needs and distracting desires.

In our consumer culture, we're bombarded with advertising and marketing messages that induce us to believe we will be fitter, happier, more productive, and ultimately more complete if only we take advantage of this once-in-a-lifetime offer of a steam-cleaning mop with three free replacement heads and an attachment for bringing a shine to horses' hooves (not available in stores). We don't *need* this crap, but the psychology of the ads compels us to believe we *want* it and must have it immediately. When we actually encounter a product or technology that genuinely enriches our lives, we don't realize how much we needed it until after we've seen it. We're often not aware we have a problem until we've been shown how to solve it. The ability to spot these occluded problems is another of the product manager's most important skills.

To return for a moment to the ancient Greeks, we can take a page from the teachings of Socrates, famous for his method of questioning. Socrates was having nothing of the Oracle of Delphi's pronouncements. When a friend of his, Chaerephon, asked the oracle whether there was anyone wiser than Socrates, he received the answer that there was no one wiser. Socrates, fully believing himself to know nothing, felt this simply could not be the case and so embarked on a quest to interview various experts about their chosen specialized subjects. If Socrates had conducted his investigations in the twenty-first century, one of the questions he might have sought an expert answer to is, what makes a good product? Is it beautiful, sleek design? How about the number of things it can do? Or maybe it's how well it does its job. Certainly these considerations play a part, but experience teaches us that there's one crucial characteristic that's often overlooked, without which a product will almost always fail: the product has to be *needed*.

THE HUNDRED-MILLION-DOLLAR ASSUMPTION

In January 2001, as the dot-com bubble was deflating,* journalist Steve Kemper woke up one day to find that he'd indirectly caused a feeding frenzy of speculation and rumor among the tech community. He discovered that someone had leaked the proposal for his next book to the (now defunct) website Inside.com. The book's synopsis told of how Kemper had shadowed the successful but eccentric inventor Dean Kamen on his journey to bring a world-changing innovation, referred to only by its codename, "Ginger," from the drawing board through funding and development to its launch. While the leaked proposal didn't reveal what Ginger was, tantalizingly it did include quotes from industry moguls such as Steve Jobs ("As big a deal as the PC"—in retrospect, a beautifully double-edged comment) and John

---

* Possibly while bouncing around the room making a rude, raspberry-type noise. March 10, 2000, is considered the date on which the dot-com bubble burst, coinciding with NASDAQ's peak at 5408.60, double what it had been a year previously, and a level still not matched—at the time of writing in May 2014, at least. http://finance.yahoo.com/q/bc?s=^IXIC&t=my&l=off&z=l&q=l&c=.

Doerr, the venture capitalist behind Netscape and Amazon ("Maybe bigger than the Internet"). Spurred on, the tech world soon dug up the patents Kamen had filed for Ginger entitled "Personal Mobility Vehicles and Methods."[1] With the dot-com bonfire of the vanities already burning well out of control, each revelation simply tossed on more fuel, triggering an explosion of speculation throughout the tech community about Ginger—including that it was a perpetual-motion engine or a *Star Trek*-style transporter that would beam people from place to place in the blink of an eye.[2]

Early in December 2001, after nearly a year of rampant speculation, the day of Ginger's unveiling dawned. In a world exclusive, ABC News' copresenters of *Good Morning America* would finally answer the tech community's burning question: what on earth *was* Ginger? As Kemper wrote later in his book, *Reinventing the Wheel*,

> [Kamen] was next to Diane Sawyer on *Good Morning America*, watching a sheet rise from Ginger. Standing naked in the spotlight, the machine looked anticlimactic: two wheels, a platform, and a T-bar.
>
> After a pause, [Charles] Gibson asked what it did. "It's the world's first self-balancing human transporter," said Dean, his Long Island accent still evident after nearly twenty years in New Hampshire. Gibson asked why it didn't topple over, as physics seemed to demand. "That's the invention," said Dean. "It does what a human does. It has gyros and sensors that act like your inner ear. It has a computer that does what your brain does for you. It's got motors that do what your muscles do for you. It's got tires that do what your feet do for you."[3]

Ginger turned out to be the Segway, and the device seemed to have the foundations in place for huge success. Kamen had a thoroughbred engineering background and many prior commercial successes in product invention, including a novel drug infusion pump and his impressive iBOT wheelchair, which allowed users to ascend stairs unaided. He'd even been photographed sitting in the chair shaking the hand of President Bill Clinton. In terms of technology, Segway was impressive; its ability to maintain balance on just two wheels while being piloted was indeed groundbreaking. John Doerr, Kamen's venture capital backer, predicted that the Segway would reach $1 billion in sales faster than any product had before. Kamen believed his ambitious new creation would "be to the car what the car was to the horse and buggy." His bold vision was to reinvent personal transport for the masses and change the world.

So why aren't we all now gliding around on these two-wheeled marvels of modern engineering? Let's return to *Good Morning America*, where we left off a moment ago. Again according to Kemper,

> [Diane] Sawyer had been silent, staring at Ginger. "I'm tempted to say, 'That's *it*?'" she blurted. "But that *can't* be *it*."
>
> She didn't understand what she was looking at. She couldn't see the 90 percent of Ginger's story hidden below the surface, and didn't know about the intense, ragged process that had moved this invention from idea to marketplace.[4]

Sure, there was the odd glitch to iron out, such as its propensity to throw its riders roughly to the ground when its battery ran out of juice. President George W. Bush deftly demonstrated the effect by falling over the handlebars while attempting a vacation excursion.

This didn't mean the Segway's design was fundamentally flawed. That could be fixed. The bigger problem had to do with Sawyer's underwhelmed "That's *it*?" reaction. Many other people had the same first impression. Segway simply couldn't live up to Ginger's hype.

But the misfire was rooted in much deeper causes than the buildup. Perhaps Kamen should have sought the advice of one of Doerr's other investment recipients, the cofounder of Netscape, Marc Andreessen: "In a great market—a market with lots of real potential customers—the market pulls product out of the startup...the #1 company-killer is lack of market."[5]

(Courtesy of Reuters/Jim Bourg)

At the time, Doerr estimated the size of the transportation market to be over $300 billion.[6] In hindsight, we might speculate that his prediction that the Segway would rapidly garner $1 billion in sales* was

---

* Purely as an aside, *Grand Theft Auto V* (a headline-grabbing video game) made over $1 billion in the *three days* following its release. With its creator's investment of reportedly between $200 million and $250 million, it just goes to show—twelve years on from Segway—that the right product in the right market can achieve astonishingly rapid commercial success. http://www.reuters.com/article/2013/09/20/entertainment-us-taketwo-gta-idUSBRE98J0O820130920.

fueled more by his fervent desire to recoup a significant chunk of the $38 million his investment firm had sunk into the Segway so far.[7]

You'd think that startups and more established companies alike would have learned their lesson by now, yet this "top-down" approach of assessing market opportunity still regularly rears its ugly head. "The total market is worth billions, so if we can secure just 0.1 percent market share, we'll all be multimillionaires by Christmas," goes the ever-optimistic pitch. Such pronouncements tend to have no more reliability than Socrates credited the Delphic Oracle with.

The sad truth is that far too many products are launched according to the three-step business plan of the crafty creatures known as the Underpants Gnomes, introduced by the ingenious creators of *South Park* in their off-the-wall "Gnomes" episode:

Phase 1	Phase 2	Phase 3
Collect underpants	**?**	Profit

Kamen and Doerr's business strategy with the Segway was based on a number of assumptions. One was that the target market would immediately recognize the value in the product or service being offered, and so customers would flock to buy and use it. It's an easy trap to fall into, particularly for technology- or engineering-led companies, which believe that the market will appreciate the complexity/elegance/shininess of a product and purchase it purely on those merits. The harsh reality for the Segway was that it was solving a problem that people simply didn't have. It was a textbook example of the proverbial solution in search of a problem. If people wanted a means of transport that could convey them short distances at a maximum speed of twelve miles per hour, they could already use a bicycle. Walking could get them there just about as well. Screw it, given the price tag of $4,950 and up for a Segway, they could even take taxicabs for such trips and still save quite a bit of cash. It's very difficult to be successful with any new product that doesn't compete favorably with the incumbent solution, especially one as effective as *having legs*. The market Kamen and Doerr were aiming for—pretty much everyone—simply didn't *need* the Segway.

Kamen also seems to have assumed that he was representative of his target market, that everyone would think the same way he did. Maybe he envisaged a throng of the environmentally conscious who would appreciate the favor they were doing the world by eschewing their fossil-fuel-burning cars for a more energy-efficient electric vehicle, their enjoyment of the journey buoyed by their ongoing delight in the elegant engineering of the Segway. And, in fairness, there probably *was* such a group of tech-savvy people out there in Silicon Valley who shared Kamen's love of technology and the product's environmental benefits, disliked walking and cycling, and had enough disposable cash to afford a Segway. But they comprised only a small niche. How many other similar potential customers were really out there—and what steps had Kamen taken to validate his and Doerr's assumption that so many other people would want to buy one? Maybe that was the second error—to vastly overestimate the size of their target market.

There was one more assumption that Kamen and Doerr should have challenged before building and launching: that customers would be *allowed* to ride their Segways. When they launched, it was illegal to ride the Segway on the sidewalk in thirty-two U.S. states and the District of Columbia.[8] And since the top speed was twelve miles per hour, customers were unlikely to risk their necks dodging traffic in the road. In the United Kingdom, where existing laws prevented Segways from being ridden in the road, a judge ruled in 2011 that they were also illegal on the pavement (what we call the sidewalk over here),[9] meaning people could only use their Segways on private land. To Segway's credit, a massive lobbying campaign spearheaded by Brian Toohey, the company's VP of regulatory affairs, did succeed in changing the U.S. state laws to permit Segways to be ridden on sidewalks.

I could almost forgive Kamen and Doerr their oversight but for the fact that Jeff Bezos, Amazon's CEO, had questioned this very assumption[10] when he and Steve Jobs met them over a year before they launched Segway. Don't you think it would have been wiser to have checked the legality of the product *before* burning through $100 million of research and development investment?

As we saw earlier, assumptions are uncertainties and uncertainties yield risks. The assumption that the Segway would be legal to ride led to a costly lobbying campaign to change state laws. Facebook's assumption that smartphone customers would want Facebook Home at the center of their mobile experience also turned out to be an expensive mistake. So how can you prevent a similar Segway-sized screwup with your own product?

In short, you need to check your assumptions and reduce your risks *before* you get to the expensive part of developing your product. Launching a new product is always going to involve risk. At the outset of any new product journey, one of the biggest challenges for a product manager (or the startup founder fulfilling that role) is the amount of uncertainty. Uncertainty comes from your lack of information and all the implicit and explicit assumptions you're making. You might have spotted a potentially lucrative problem to solve, but at the early stages you know little about the people in the market you'll be catering to. You may have a vague idea of what your product would need to do to solve the problem, but you're lacking in the detail of how it will do this. All this uncertainty translates into risk, and risk in turn can translate into cost and can account for the overall success or failure of the product.

Risk is simply a probability of something bad happening (or good—in which case we call it opportunity). Whenever you clamber into your car and take a ride, there is a small risk you'll have an accident. Being a competent, attentive, and experienced driver allows you to read the road well. But even with that experience, you will surely get in an accident if you wear a blindfold while driving. Leaping into the creation of a product on gut instinct alone, without doing research and rigorously putting your assumptions to the test, is the business equivalent of driving blindfolded. There is a series of questions you should ask about any product before you get into the development process.

IS THERE A MARKET IN YOUR GAP?

I was chatting with someone recently about what it meant to be a product manager in a startup in terms of the day-to-day role and whether it differed much from working in a larger company. In a startup, I suggested, money is particularly tight, so a product manager has even more responsibility than usual to ensure that by the time the expensive development work starts, the product research has been done. It's crucial to have a solid idea of what the product needs to be to solve the market problem identified. Of course, I'm not suggesting that profligacy is to be encouraged in larger companies, either. In my experience, the cost overheads of doing any development work have a nasty habit of increasing with the size of the company due to process and bureaucracy, no matter how hard you try to rein them in. That's not to mention how commonly a product direction is shunted off track on the whim of a meddling senior executive who thinks the idea he had in the shower that morning trumps the findings from market research. In any situation, you are responsible for being prudent with the cash spent on development.

First and foremost, the best thing a product manager can do is challenge the rationale for a new product, no matter how good the idea may seem. Establish whether the gap identified in the market of products has a market in the gap. A product gap in the market is decidedly not the same thing as a market of consumers hungry for you to fill that gap; some product gaps exist for good reasons.

You've got to unpack the product idea and consider a key set of questions about the problem the product is supposed to be solving:

» **Is it pervasive?** Who specifically has the problem, and does it affect lots of people?
» **Is it urgent?** Do those people need the problem to be solved right away, or can they wait?

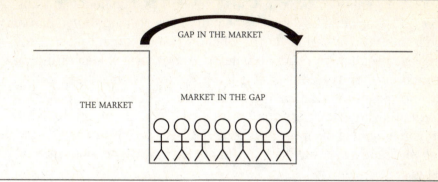

Are there real customers in the market gap you've spotted? (Image concept courtesy of General Assembly)

> » **Is it complex?** Are they able to solve the problem for themselves, or can someone else solve it for them?
> » **Is it valuable?** How painful is the problem for them, and would they be willing to part with hard cash to solve it?
> » **Is it profitable?** Will it cost us more or less than the value of the problem to solve it?

You've got to be working to figure out whether there are real people in the identified market segment who will truly see the value of the product—and whether there are enough of them. The ideal is to identify a pervasive problem, one that affects an entire market segment. If you're seeing that the problem you're trying to solve affects only some of the market you're looking at, it may well be that you haven't segmented the market enough, meaning you haven't noted some differences between groups of people in the market, maybe between people of different ages or different degrees of comfort with new technology. You need to start channeling your inner Sherlock Holmes and analyze how people *with* the problem are different from those *without* it.

Segmenting the target market in this way may mean that you end up with a very small niche, which may not necessarily be a bad thing. A narrower focus can be a plus, especially for a startup. If you can fully understand the dynamics of the whole market segment most likely to buy your product, you stand a much better chance of succeeding in it. From the beachhead you establish there, you can then start to branch out and target adjacent markets. It is far better to have a few thousand enthused customers than a hundred thousand indifferent ones. But you may also discover that your market opportunity is so specific that you'll only ever have a handful of customers—or sometimes even just one.

The Large Hadron Collider at CERN is a gargantuan, subterranean, doughnut-shaped proton smasher that has been used to prove the existence of the elusive Higgs boson, among other things. The LHC has around it ninety superconductive magnets chilled to close to absolute zero that it uses to accelerate two beams of particles to near light speed[11] in opposite directions within its torus shape. Even though the subatomic particles flying around the loop have minuscule mass, they're traveling so fast that the collision between the two particle beams is like two passenger trains, each moving at 95 mph (or around 150 kph),[12] hitting each other head-on—a lot of smashing will occur. When a catastrophic leak of supercooled helium occurred ten days after initial switch-on in September 2008, the ultrafast particle beams broke free of their magnetic constraints (like speeding trains on the loose) and severely damaged the LHC.* Many of its ninety magnets had to be replaced over the course of the following year.[13] CERN now keeps a full replacement set in case something similar happens again.

---

* It turns out that this was not an isolated event. More recently, a pigeon nearly caused the same thing to happen again by dropping a piece of baguette onto one of the supercooled magnets, raising its temperature above the point where it ceases to be a superconductor. This containment failure would have resulted in similar damage were it not for the safety valves that had been added since the last incident. A pigeon. Seriously? See: Lewis Page, "Large Hadron Collider Scuttled by Birdy Baguette-Bomber," *The Register*, November 5, 2009, http://www.theregister.co.uk/2009/11/05/lhc_bread_bomb_dump_incident/.

If you were the product manager at the company manufacturing those specialized superconductive magnets, your entire market would be that one customer.

That might be fine with a high-ticket item like those magnets, but if your product isn't sufficiently high-value that you'll turn a profit even with just a few customers, you should reevaluate whether you're being too specific with the problem you're solving, and even whether it's worth trying to solve the problem in the first place.

It must be said that those who have come up with the product idea may not be overwhelmed with joy in response to your feedback. Especially when advising startups, don't be surprised if founders react defensively. After all, the product they envision is their baby. But just keep in mind that the massive favor you're doing them is to give them the greatest chance of success and thus to reduce the amount of their limited funding that will go up in smoke for no return.

DOES THE CONSUMER HAVE A MOTIVATION TO BUY?

As the Segway demonstrated so deftly, product ideas often fall down because their developers fail to assess whether customers will be sufficiently motivated to actually use the product. Many product creators I've spoken with confuse the *means* with the *end*. They think people will want to use the product just because it exists. "We're going to create a new marketplace for exchanging services," they'll say. "Once we have a few hundred users we'll be able to use their subscription fees to fund further growth and services."

The flaw here is thinking that users will turn up and use the marketplace just because the creators built it. Or made it social. Or gamified it. Sadly, this is not *Field of Dreams* and they're not Kevin Costner. If you build it, the users will not come—unless they have a strong motivation to do so. The problem you're solving has to be sufficiently painful, urgent, and difficult to solve by some other means for the potential customers you've identified to buy. You must be tough-minded in asking yourself, *What's in it for them?*

The danger of operating by wish fulfillment is especially prevalent among startups. One startup I came across was proposing a marketplace for woodworkers to connect with a larger potential customer base of people needing home improvement work, such as help assembling a flat-pack kitchen. The reasoning went that woodworkers would prefer to have a steady stream of jobs set up for them, rather than having to waste time on the phone talking to customers about jobs and selling their services. Think Uber, but for carpentry. Using this as an example, let's work through our questions:

Who specifically has the problem, and does it affect many people? The premise is that woodworkers have the problems of wanting a steadier stream of work and not wanting to have to waste time on the phone with customers. We can see that the problem affects many woodworkers (or is pervasive), because many of them have no web presence or advertising in the yellow pages.

There are already a few implicit assumptions being made here—did you spot them? Firstly, do woodworkers actually want a steadier stream of work? They may be perfectly happy with the current situation. Similarly, they may not consider the time on the phone to be a waste, as it may give them an opportunity to assess the customer's needs, ask questions, and make a good first impression. Also, is it necessarily the case that woodworkers without a web presence or advertising in the yellow pages receive less business than they want? They could be receiving work through word-of-mouth referral or by smartly targeting people who may need to have some fix-ups done, such as those putting their homes on the market.

Do they need this problem to be solved right away, or can they wait? It's not that urgent. Woodworkers have been perfectly able to find business up until now without this new web marketplace, so in the absence of any major market-changing event, they can probably hang on for a bit longer.

Are they able to solve the problem for themselves, or can someone else solve it for them? An individual woodworker can be in only one place at a time, so he needs only enough work to keep him busy and doesn't necessarily need to target too wide an area. He's able to advertise his services in a relatively cheap and direct manner through letter drops, ads in local shops, and so on. There are also websites that allow customers to recommend handymen to others. So it seems that there are already workable alternative solutions to the problem that do the job well enough.

How painful is the problem for them, and would they be willing to part with hard cash to solve it? The problem doesn't seem to be painful enough for the woodworkers. As a result, it's unlikely they would part with much cash, unless they happened to be failing to find enough work and the product really could guarantee them a steady stream of jobs. But perhaps there's a segment who *are* really struggling with the problem, and maybe that segment represents a sufficient market. How could you find out for sure?

Will it cost more or less than the value of the problem to solve it? You will be charging a fee for the service, and the question is, how much will customers be willing to pay? That depends in part on the costs versus the benefits. The subscription fee each woodworker pays must make the company some profit over the cost of servicing the account. If the fee is too low, every new subscriber will result in a net loss. If it's too high, the woodworkers won't see sufficient advantage in paying for it.

Pricing is one of the trickiest things to get right about a new product, for many reasons. Often the price you'd like to charge is simply more than most customers are willing to pay. While I was working at Iron Mountain, the pricing of one of the company's products was insufficient to generate a viable margin of profit. The product in question was a service that continuously backed up consumers' laptops to storage servers in the cloud. The profit margin on the service was tight even according to the business plan, and the profit was contingent on the service compressing the customers' files before they were archived. For some reason, however, this wasn't happening. So the slim margin was eaten up by the company's larger-than-expected storage costs. The growing "success" of the product translated into increasing loss. It should come as no surprise that Iron Mountain eventually sold off their digital archival division to Autonomy[14] in order to refocus on their physical storage services.

Pricing a product deserves a book in its own right, so a few short lines here will not do the topic justice. Finding the right price points for your product relies on having a great depth of understanding about its context: its potential customers and their expectations, its fixed and variable costs, its competitors, the life cycle stage of the product and its market, perhaps even the product's relative standing within a larger portfolio, as well as many other considerations. A product manager is uniquely placed to weigh up these different factors—he is one of the few people in a company whose job it is to have such a detailed knowledge. There are also many different pricing strategies, some of which are more applicable to certain industries than others. You wouldn't expect to pay by the minute to read a book, nor would you expect to pay more for a subway ticket because you happened to have the train car to yourself. For more detail on the variety of pricing strategies available to you, the psychology behind them, and their application, take a look at the comprehensive list I've included for you in the notes.[15]

One of the reasons people often find product pricing so hard is that they're struggling to establish the product's value to its customers. This is why it's so important to understand how painful and how urgent the problem is. In the classes I teach, I illustrate the point by picking up a student's half-finished bottle of water. I turn to another student and ask how much she'd pay me for it. Not unreasonably, the answer is "Nothing." Fair enough, I say. I then ask her to imagine she's been trekking across the expanse of the Sahara desert with the relentless sun beating down on her. It's been several hours since she ran out of water and her tongue is dry and swollen. Like a product manager genie, I present to her the same secondhand bottle of water, now magically transformed into a life saver. How much would she pay me for it now? "Everything I have" is the typical response. If you can time your request for payment to the point when your customer recognizes the value of your product most, you'll find people are far more willing to part with their hard-earned cash.

WANTS VERSUS NEEDS

Most of us are pretty good at recognizing our needs—but often only with the benefit of hindsight: a sudden downpour makes me wish I'd brought my umbrella; ominous clicking noises from my laptop's hard drive remind me that I really need to start backing up my work. It's vital never to make assumptions about customers' needs and whether they will recognize them. It was nearly fifty years after the invention of the tin can that someone invented the can opener. One issue is that our needs are often latent or unexpressed. We may experience a need as a yawning gap in our lives that wears on us but that we haven't clearly identified, such as the desire to do a good job, be successful, or know we're on the right track with something.

Abraham Maslow famously wrote about people having a hierarchy of needs, starting with those required for basic physiological health, such as breathing, food, and water; progressing to needs for love and for satisfaction in our lives; and moving on to "self-actualization," which can be achieved, for example, through exercising our creativity and problem-solving skills. Our survival needs are obvious, but needs that relate more to the quality of our lives are easier to neglect or sublimate.

It can also be easy to confuse wants with needs. I may *want* that second slice of baked cheesecake, but my spreading girth will attest to the fact that I certainly don't *need* it. Wants are not the same as needs, but we often mistake them as such. This is why it's sometimes difficult to read between the lines of the explicit *wants* expressed by your potential customers in order to latch on to their actual *needs*, which may be implicit ones they're not themselves aware of.

We can all get caught up in thinking some cool new product will serve needs we don't have. I was having trouble getting my modestly sized car into my snugly proportioned garage. As a creative (and slightly geeky) product manager, I thought for a while that I could perhaps craft some kind of complex parking sensor and camera array that would help me park more easily. Of course what I really needed was either a smaller car or a bigger garage, or to learn how to reverse-park better.

We're all inclined to think we need things we want—until, that is, we're asked to pay for them. Then we suddenly don't want them anymore. So learning to delve more deeply into the problems people truly need to solve and why (whether or not they understand the need yet), rather than putting too much emphasis on what they might say they want, is an important skill for a product manager to develop. This is why we need to know our customers' needs better than they know them themselves.

IS THE PRODUCT OFFERING A REAL-WORLD BENEFIT?

As with wants and needs, people also seem to find it hard to spot the difference between a *feature* and a *benefit*. So many product descriptions and marketing pitches demonstrate this when they focus primarily on the product features and perhaps mention a benefit right at the end. Have you ever had the misfortune to be accosted by a telesales person whose entire selling technique consisted of listing all the things the product could do, how many buttons and accessories it had, and how capacious its memory was? There's a reason why this pitch fell flat: *features don't resonate with the buyer, only benefits do.* A better approach would have been for the telesales person to describe what real-world, emotional impact the product would have on you.

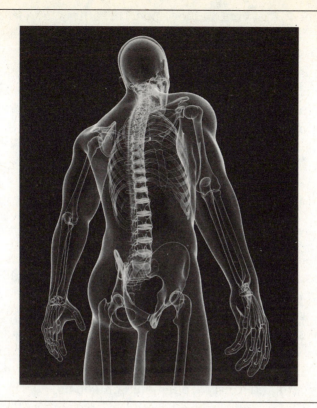

(Courtesy of Dreamstime.com)

Occasionally, a product stands out because its benefits are expressed well and resonate with the potential buyer. As a biker, I regularly find myself in stores that sell motorcycle gear. There's a brand called Knox that makes safety armor, the padded inserts that protect knees, shoulders, and elbows when motorcycle and rider part company unexpectedly. I was browsing a motorcycle store one day and came across Knox's products. In the midst of their display was a life-sized cardboard model of a human spine, with arrows pointing to the vertebrae that control movement, breathing, and so on. Next to the model I saw a small placard advertising their new back protector that highlighted how it protected each region of the spine. Being an old traditionalist at heart, I quite enjoy moving and breathing (and referring back to Maslow, they're fairly fundamental needs), so the benefit of avoiding spinal damage in a motorcycle accident resonated strongly with me. With that seed planted in my mind, every time I thought about going riding without a back protector, I was reminded of how much I enjoy moving and breathing. I now own—and wear—a Knox back protector.

There is a simple technique you can use to home in on the benefits of a product versus its features or characteristics. Every time you describe what you think is a benefit, ask yourself repeatedly: "So what?" Essentially, when you get to the point that you can't sensibly ask the question any longer because the benefit is self-evident, you're there. Say you're selling mortgage loans. Is a loan at a good rate really the extent of the benefit you're offering? By asking themselves "So what?" banks have started to market their mortgages not as a means to buy a house, but as a way to enable a shorter commute and make it home in time to read your child a bedtime story. Benefits matter to us in the real world and exert an emotional pull on us.

In contrast, the *features* of a product or service are the means by which it helps the user to realize its benefits. My motorcycle would not allow me to experience the benefit of the enjoyment I get from chasing up a winding road if it didn't have the features of quick steering and a responsive engine. Similarly, any benefit of enjoyment it brings would come to an abrupt and sticky end if it lacked the key feature of brakes. Another way to illustrate the relationship between benefits and features is with Trello,[16] a tool I often use to manage product backlogs for my clients. It's like a virtual set of sticky notes on a board and is particularly helpful when I'm coordinating remote development teams that can't see the more typical sprint board. The chart shows the difference between a benefit (the answer to the question, "So what?") and a feature (which describes what the product does).

Benefit (The "So What")		Feature (The "What")
People don't need to be in the same room to see the board	because	it's web-based, so people can view it online.
People can start using it quickly, a must for me on short projects	because	it's intuitive and doesn't require lengthy training.
I can use the same tool on different projects easily	because	it doesn't impose any specific method or process.

Benefits are the real-world outcomes of using a product that resonate emotionally; and *features* are the capabilities or characteristics of a product that allow users to realize those benefits.

One of the pitfalls in product development is focusing too much on cool features that may not offer actual benefits. Take the case of the Rong Zun 758 Razor mobile phone. It included many good features, such as a touch screen and dual SIM card slots, but it also featured an actual razor—an automatic shaver at the base of the phone.[17] How many people really want to shave with their phone? Needless to say, this feature was not widely adopted by mobile phone makers.

It's important to always keep the distinction between benefits and features in mind to make sure you don't fall down this rabbit hole.

DON'T ASSUME, CHECK

There are many ways of becoming aware of hidden assumptions you're making and testing them. A good method to start with is to find your most honest (or cynical) friend. Sit down with her and describe your product's proposition in as much detail as you can. Her job is to write down all the assumptions you're making, whether implicitly or explicitly. For each, she should ask you, "How do you know that x is the case?" If you don't have evidence to support each assumption, you're going to need to find some. This will inevitably lead you to create such a long, sprawling list that it will have you doubting whether you can safely assume that up is up and down is down. So your next step is to prioritize the most important assumptions to check. These are the riskiest ones that stand to have the greatest negative (or positive) impact on your product. In the case of Segway, one of the riskiest assumptions was that the machine would be legal to ride, and we know how well that turned out.

There are several ways in which you can test your assumptions. The scale and method of the tests will vary, but the objective is always the same: to reduce the risk of your product idea by gathering some hard evidence to support your decisions. You could run surveys to verify that your target market is in fact thirtysomething professionals with disposable income, or multivariate tests to discover the optimal combination of size, color, and placement of the "Buy now" button to maximize the number of purchases made, or more complex experiments to check whether people actually have the problem you think your product is solving in the first place.

Of the techniques you can use to test your assumptions, creating a minimum viable product (MVP) is particularly fashionable right now. An MVP is typically an early release of a product intended to check how effectively it solves a market problem. It is deliberately kept as minimal as possible to avoid wasting time and effort developing something that may fail to hit the mark. However, the technique is misapplied quite often. The concept of an MVP, as most people think of it, comes primarily from Eric Ries's book, *The Lean Startup*. Among the principles he introduces, Ries advocates a cyclical approach, *Build—Measure—Learn*, to be done on as rapid a turnaround as possible, with some companies (including his own) managing an exhausting fifty iterations in a day. Despite being minimal, a true MVP also has to be *commercially viable*, not a semifunctional heap of junk. People should find it sufficiently desirable that they will part with hard cash to have it, otherwise you're not going to learn whether your product is solving a sufficiently valuable problem. Building an MVP can be expensive and time-consuming, but it's often an important step in testing user responses. Entrepreneur Richard Branson's MVP for Virgin Atlantic required him to lease, fit out, and operate a single aircraft so he could learn whether his target customers would pay for the glamorous travel experience he provided. His MVP was as minimal an experiment as possible for his market, but was still costly and complex by software standards.

Where software developers start to go off track is that they assume the *build* part of Ries's cycle always means *write code*. The thinking behind the methodology is to learn as much as possible, but people forget that the intention is also to learn as cheaply, quickly, and easily as possible. Companies squeeze both the timeline and costs in product development and then attempt to legitimize a barely functioning prototype by incorrectly calling it an MVP. Then, when the product inevitably fails, they don't use the opportunity to learn anything that will make their next iteration more successful. There often is no second iteration. In this respect, MVP has become the new beta program (another method of testing an early product iteration with real customers that was similarly abused). This is one reason it's a good idea to test aspects of your product with simpler prototypes before you reach the MVP stage. If you happen to have some ultraefficient developer-designers, they may indeed be able to create a high-fidelity prototype very quickly. But it may be cheaper, quicker, and just as effective to sketch the design out with a Sharpie and test that paper mockup with a few people instead.

The purpose of testing is to *learn* something so you can make improvements. The less you have invested in a version you're testing, the easier the product will be to change. That doesn't mean your thinking about what you want to learn from testing should be rough, though. You won't learn much if you don't set out with a clear idea of what you think your test will prove and what evidence would constitute the proof. It's a good idea to be as specific as you can. If your assumption is that your customers will use your product more at certain times of the day, specify in your hypothesis which users you're talking about and what times of day in particular, and quantify how much will satisfy the definition of "more"—does it need to be 5, 50, or

500 percent more? Then you need to devise and run a quick, cheap, and simple check that will allow you to test that hypothesis.

My students often struggle to think of the most straightforward ways to check their assumptions. So I ask them how long they think it took Google to prototype Glass, the company's wearable computer. The guesses usually range from months to years. When Tom Chi from Google X, Google's not-very-top-secret special projects lab, set out to test whether Project Glass would work, he knocked together an initial prototype in just a few minutes with modeling wire and blobs of Play-Doh for weight. He learned from this quick usability test how much the unit could weigh before it began to hurt people's ears.[18] He also learned that the bridge of the nose could tolerate more weight than the ears before it became uncomfortable. This is why Google Glass is designed slightly nose-heavy.

Chi and his team also thought it would be cool to be able to interact with Glass using *Minority Report*-style hand gestures, so a couple hours of rapid prototyping later, with some fishing twine connecting the users' wrists via pulleys to levers allowing them to click mouse buttons, they'd rigged up a system that allowed users to change slides on a projected screen by gesturing with their hands. What they learned from this is that if you hold your hands above your heart for more than a few minutes, lactic acid starts to build up and your shoulders become tired and painful pretty quickly (try it). If, however, you keep your hands below your heart, you can hold them there pretty much forever. From this experiment, Chi learned that a *Minority Report*-style interface wouldn't work. To feel right, the hand interaction needed to be in the field of vision (looking slightly up, not down), but since they'd discovered this would be painful to use for extended periods of time, they abandoned the idea. A few hours of prototyping had saved the cost and effort of developing a gesture-driven interface for Google Glass that was never going to work.

There's no right or wrong way to test your hypotheses as long as you isolate the thing you're testing so that coincidental factors don't mislead you, and you learn something from the experiment. As you'll read in plenty of books about software product development, there are many specific techniques for checking your assumptions, including wireframes (drawings of the pages of your app), surveys, prototypes, and usability tests. As a product manager you'll definitely want to become familiar with all of these, so that you can either do them yourself or have someone on your team do so, and it's a good idea to take the time to read about them in-depth or take a class about them. But as Tom Chi showed, even if you're building something as complex as a wearable computer built into glasses, it's also a great idea to run a quick, cheap, and easy test to validate your assumptions. You can do it for any product if you think creatively enough.

You don't even need to write a line of code to build a version of your product suitable for testing. If you wanted to create a new dog-walking website and app that matches up people who don't have time to walk their dogs with people who can do it for them, your MVP to test the concept could be to run the service for real with a telephone and an Excel spreadsheet and charge for it. This is sometimes referred to as a *concierge MVP*—just as a concierge performs services on behalf of his guests, you're manually carrying out all the tasks that your product would do. From this you'd be able to learn a huge amount about your target market, different users' habits and concerns, and how much you could reasonably charge for the service. In this scenario, all you're doing when creating the website and app is automating the aspects that won't scale if they continue to be done manually. You should try to avoid expensive development at all costs while you're still testing whether the bare-bones product concept works.

Take the case of the Pebble watch, another piece of wearable tech, which has an e-paper face and connects to your smartphone. When its developers ran into a wall with venture capitalists who didn't believe enough in the product to offer any more funding, they didn't give up.[19] Instead they launched a Kickstarter campaign to establish whether its potential customers would put their money where their mouths were. The video they posted on Kickstarter was their MVP—by mocking up how the Pebble watch would work before they'd built one, its creators were able to test their assumption that people would part with hard cash for it. Against a funding target of $100,000, Pebble raised $10.3 million in pledges in thirty-seven days[20]—not bad going.

The Pebble watch (Courtesy of Pebble Technology Corp.)

Use prototypes, mockups, and other small tests to check specific aspects of your product, as with Google Glass, then when you're ready to test how customers will experience your product experience as a whole, move onto an MVP, just as Virgin Atlantic and Pebble did.

These rapid experiments help you make small course corrections—or *pivots*—to your product's direction. Did you know that pivoting (in the *Lean Startup* sense) comes from basketball? When a player has the ball, he can pivot around one foot to make a pass. But the key thing is that he has one foot planted where he was and the other pointing him in a new direction. In the same way, when we think of a pivot in product terms, we're changing direction but still keeping one foot where we started. We want to build on what we've learned so far. What some people wrongly call a pivot is the equivalent of taking the basketball and walking off the court and out of the stadium to play an entirely different game. In the same way, embarking on a completely new product idea is not a small course correction—it means starting from scratch with a new set of assumptions to test out, and losing the benefits of everything learned about their target market and product until that point. Consider that the hugely successful lubricant WD-40 is so named because the final product was the fortieth incremental tweak to the formula its developer, chemist Norm Larsen, made.

WHEN TO MAKE AN MVP

As we saw earlier, people find it hard to recognize they have a need until they experience something that satisfies it. Once a product solves their problem especially well, they'll find they can't live without it. This is one reason creating an actual working version to test can be so valuable. In contrast with the little course corrections that small experiments help with, the purpose of an MVP is to help you learn whether the broader product vision is sound by trying it out with people Ries calls "earlyvangelists," identified years earlier by Geoffrey Moore, author of the business classic *Crossing the Chasm*, as the "early adopters." These are the kind of people who once took a long, hard look at some moldy, solidified milk and thought to themselves, "I reckon I can eat that and not die. I shall call it 'cheese.'" The reason an MVP can be minimal is that these early adopters are enthusiasts who can look beyond the missing features and rough edges to see the inherent potential in a first commercial release, then gain social capital with their peers by showing how cutting-edge they are. Early adopters get a kick out of being the trailblazers.

It should be said that the concept of the MVP is by no means a new one. In January 2001, Apple released the first version of iTunes, a piece of software that allowed Mac users to convert (or "rip") audio CDs into compressed audio files.[21] At the time, successfully ripping music still required a reasonable amount of technical know-how, and so had been a pastime almost exclusively for enthusiasts. By making the process simpler and more user-friendly, iTunes presented Apple with the opportunity to test out whether digital music would be popular with a wider market. Arguably, on the basis of the success and feedback from the launch of iTunes with Apple's early adopters, Apple created and launched the very first generation of iPod just a few months later, in October 2001.

The first-generation iPod (Courtesy of Apple)

iTunes was one of Apple's major experiments, a way for the company to test whether it should enter an entirely new market. All iTunes could do at launch was rip and organize a library of music—there was no iTunes Store or even an iPod to send the music to (yet). The hypothesis Apple was testing was that the mainstream market was ready for digital music. So it took the quickest, easiest, and arguably cheapest route for its minimum viable product to test this out. It didn't invest thousands of development hours building its own software from scratch, but instead adapted a piece of software it had recently acquired called SoundJam MP[22] into the first version of iTunes.

The first generation iPod was Apple's next major experiment, and again we can think of it as an MVP. Under Steve Jobs's direct supervision the iPod was evolved from reference hardware Apple acquired from PortalPlayer.[23] It was compatible with Macs only and had just five gigabytes of storage ("a thousand songs in your pocket"), a mechanical (not touch-sensitive) scroll wheel, and a chunky monochrome screen. It was a stark contrast to the button-rich, unintuitive MP3 players already on the market, which had been designed by techies for techies. Yet it still came with a price tag of $399—hefty in 2001. Early adopters pulled about 125,000 first-generation iPods out of Apple's hands in the two months between the October launch and Christmas that year.[24] Tellingly, by December third-party developers had already started to create software equivalent to iTunes that would allow PC users to join the iPod party. Remember what Andreessen said earlier in the chapter? *In a great market . . . the market pulls product out of the startup.* Demand for the iPod was clear among early adopters, at least. Apple had tapped into an unmet need, and both its traditional customers (Mac users) and new ones (PC users) were willing to part with a premium to solve their problem. Its challenge was then to determine what the "whole product"[25] would need to be in order to take the iPod mainstream successfully.

HOW TO DELIGHT YOUR CUSTOMERS

It's one thing to understand how to check your assumptions and validate your product concept with an MVP, but how do you decide, from all the possible features your product could have, which to include?

Back in the 1980s, Noriaki Kano, professor emeritus of the Tokyo University of Science, devised a model for assessing customer satisfaction that proposed that not all features are born equal. Through a process of questioning that came to be known as the Kano model, individual product features can be ranked and differentiated depending on whether consumers consider them to be baseline features, linear satisfiers, or delighters.

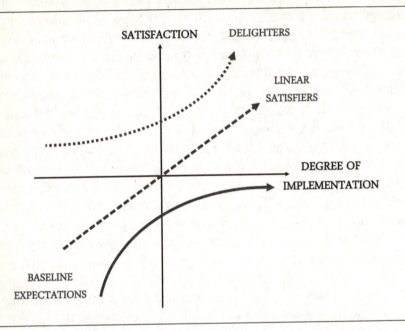

The Kano model simplified

Baseline features are those a product must have at a minimum to be considered a contender. A hotel room needs to provide a bed and a bathroom at minimum. While their presence doesn't really affect customer satisfaction, their absence will really reduce it. How annoyed would you be if your hotel room didn't have a bed?

Linear satisfiers (sometimes referred to as *performance characteristics*) are a case of "the more the better." The more of this kind of feature you have, the more satisfied you are—and the less you have, the less satisfied you are. You might consider a tablet device that offers twice as much storage space for photos, videos, and music proportionally more satisfying than another model. And you'd probably be less satisfied with a tablet that offered only half as much storage.

And then you have delighters. These are the kinds of features that vastly increase consumers' satisfaction, but whose absence doesn't detract from it. This is essentially because these features tap into users' latent needs—the users weren't even aware that they *had* the need until they saw the feature. Delight can come from unexpected places: it could be the restaurant that surprises you with a round of drinks on the house because you've been kept waiting for your meal, or an aspect of a product that is so much fun to use that it transcends its basic utility. Sometimes it's something that makes you feel special by letting you in on the joke or secret, as neatly demonstrated by fruit smoothie maker Innocent Drinks (see photo).

Innocent's delightful smoothie carton (Courtesy of Duncan Cumming and Innocent Drinks)

As you might imagine, good products have a combination of all three types of features. They tend to be priced in proportion to the linear satisfiers, and the products that have more delighters tend to be the ones that people will recommend to each other most. Of course, some products fail to have any delightful characteristics whatsoever, as seems to be the case with most business-to-business (B2B) software, so these are markets ripe for disruption by a delightful product.

But note that there is one consideration to be aware of regarding adding features that start off as delighters—they can quickly become linear satisfiers, then baseline expectations over time. Think about touch screens on mobile phones, for example. Apple's iPhone was not the first mobile with a touch screen instead of a keypad, but its elegance in construction, feel, and use made it a thing of delight when it was unveiled—it blew the competition away and set a new benchmark. But it didn't take long for competitors to replicate the iPhone's touch screen, turning it first into a linear satisfier (the bigger and higher resolution the screen, the better) and soon after into a baseline expectation for all mobile phones. Delighters won't delight forever.

It's also tough to keep finding new ways to delight your customers. With each progressive generation of iPhone, the wow factor has diminished. Nor is it the answer just to keep throwing in new features in the hope that more is better—the product will quickly become an unusable, chaotic mess. The Wenger Giant Swiss Army Knife includes eighty-seven implements, from a cigar cutter to a fish scaler to a wood saw, but weighs three pounds, so it can hardly be carried around handily. So it's not really a pocket knife anymore, is it?

Keeping the addition of features in check and making sure any feature you add serves a good purpose as well as delighting users is the way to steer the course through this challenging terrain.

TELLING STORIES

So far we've explored how products must be needed to succeed, how we must test our assumptions in order to reduce risk and determine whether our products will benefit the people in the market gap we've discovered, and how to evaluate which features to include. All of this leads us to one of the most important considerations for a product manager: you need to have a deep understanding of and empathy with your customers before you can truly say you know them and represent their needs. So how do you go about attaining this knowledge?

As is often the case with product management, the answer lies outside your four walls. You need to experience what life is like for these people, if not directly then vicariously by talking to (and shadowing, if possible) as many of them as you can. Assuming you already have an inkling of an idea for a product, you might start out by having open conversations to conduct your wide-angled market research. You could perhaps do this by having informal chats over a coffee or where potential customers work. And by "having open conversations" I really mean "listening attentively to your interviewees." Let them speak about their chosen specialized subject—themselves. This is not an opportunity to pitch your fledgling product to them or to convince them of the brilliance of your idea if they don't get it. Listen, digest, and learn. Each conversation you have will allow you to do a couple of things: first, to reinforce—or challenge—the picture you're building up about the real problem your product needs to solve, and second, to verify that you've correctly identified the people who have the problem to start with.

So far, so good. But you don't stop there. You keep having your conversations, now focusing in a little more on the group of people who you now know have the problem. You continue learning more about their daily lives, their habits, and their environment: where they tend to be and at what times of day they experience the problem. What other products do they often use? Understanding this might give you some insight into their level of technical confidence and a frame of reference for your subsequent user interface design. How do they currently work around the problem when it crops up? How effectively do they solve it? There are so many questions because you know so little. How would you know? After all, you're almost never the target user. Each insight you gain adds another brushstroke to the painting, and these seemingly random pieces of information will begin to coalesce gradually into a distinct picture of your target market. As this goes on, something else will happen: you'll start to see tribes emerging. As you understand more about the people you speak to, you'll start to realize that their needs are nuanced, not uniform, and that they naturally fall into groups with similar needs and behaviors. You'll start to identify what we call *user personas*.

Lucie McLean was born in Glasgow and now lives in Manchester, England, but she's kept her Scottish accent. She has a penchant for stylish, vintage clothing, particularly fifties chic, and can often be found kicking up flumes of champagne powder while carving down a piste on her snowboard. In her spare time, Lucie founded Powderroom,[26] which has grown into a popular community web magazine for female snowboarders. Is this beginning to conjure up a picture of Lucie in your mind's eye? Something like: active; a leader, not a follower; media-savvy? Or perhaps you envisage her in a fifties polka-dot dress on a snowboard? Either way, with a little bit of backstory, our minds will create a memorable image, something that brings a description to life. We enjoy stories with color far more than lists of dull facts. A user persona generalizes relevant, common characteristics and usual behaviors of a typical product user, much as I began to do with Lucie earlier. Personas create a narrative for your product team about your users, humanizing them and bringing them to life in a way that's more meaningful than any set of raw demographic statistics. This is why user personas are so powerful. And once you've created them, they become a kind of shorthand reference for the collection of characteristics they embody.

Below is an example of a good persona, created by UX designer Luke Miller, the author of General Assembly's book in this series on UX design, *The Practitioner's Guide to User Experience Design*.

It's best to enhance user personas with photographs of representative users. Such portraits can even tell a vivid story by themselves, because we can relate to the people and begin to empathize with them, and we can take an educated guess as to how well or badly each of them would respond to particular product features. Combine a set of photos with the

Max

Persona for a
social photo
taking app.

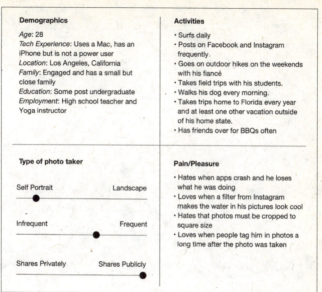

Demographics

Age: 28
Tech Experience: Uses a Mac, has an
iPhone but is not a power user
Location: Los Angeles, California
Family: Engaged and has a small but
close family
Education: Some post undergraduate
Employment: High school teacher and
Yoga instructor

Activities

• Surfs daily
• Posts on Facebook and Instagram
  frequently
• Goes on outdoor hikes on the weekends
  with his fiancé
• Takes field trips with his students.
• Walks his dog every morning.
• Takes trips home to Florida every year
  and at least one other vacation outside
  of his home state.
• Has friends over for BBQs often

Type of photo taker

Self Portrait — Landscape

Infrequent — Frequent

Shares Privately — Shares Publicly

Pain/Pleasure

• Hates when apps crash and he loses
  what he was doing
• Loves when a filter from Instagram
  makes the water in his pictures look cool
• Hates that photos must be cropped to
  square size
• Loves when people tag him in photos a
  long time after the photo was taken

A user persona should focus on details relevant to the product. (Courtesy of Luke Miller)

backstory you'll have gathered through your interviews, and you'll have a clear picture of who your users are; what habits they already have; and where, when, why, and how they'll need to use your product.

We already know that Lucie loves snowboarding—in fact, she's passionate about sports of all varieties. This is no bad thing given that she also happens to be the executive product manager at the BBC responsible for all BBC Sport's mobile websites and native apps. She oversaw the record-breaking online coverage of the 2012 Summer Olympics in London, with more than a third of the 9.5 million site visitors per day coming from mobile devices.[27] Her next challenge was to provide a platform for winter-sports lovers to engage and participate more directly with the online coverage of the 2014 Winter Olympics in Sochi. If London 2012 was all about never missing a moment, Sochi 2014 was

Users are real people, not caricatures. (Courtesy of Julian Haler)

all about sharing in the moment. Lucie uses strong narrative elements in her user personas to bring realism and humanity to them. In a talk she gave in Zurich in September 2013, she recommended following the advice of Steve Portigal not to "create distancing caricatures" of your users but instead to "look for ways to represent what you've learned [from conversations with users] in a way that maintains the messiness of actual human beings."[28] Users are real people, with hopes and fears, desires and frustrations. Crafting personas helps you keep this in mind.

MORE THAN THE VOICE OF THE CUSTOMER

With the benefit of all this valuable research we conduct with our potential future users, product managers are often the best-placed people in an organization to distill that research down into a coherent vision and plan for the product. This often leads to product managers being referred to as "the voice of the customer." But is it a helpful label? Whenever I hear it, it conjures up an image of the product manager as a ventriloquist's dummy, sitting on the customer's knee, appearing to speak independently but in fact simply saying whatever the customer wants her to. It makes people think that product managers are just a mouthpiece for information received elsewhere, making the right noises but adding nothing to the interpretation. The label "the voice of the customer" devalues what we do within an organization because it is overly reductive. Sticking with parlor tricks, "customer mind reader" may be a better description, but even that implies some kind of clever illusion on the part of product managers, as if we were cold-reading our customers by making general observations that have the ring of truth but lack any real insight or detail. So that's not quite right, either.

Our job would be a whole lot less challenging—and interesting—if everyone "knew themselves," as the inscription at Delphi urged pilgrims. As we've discussed, people don't know their own minds as well as they might think. This is why product managers need to be far more actively involved in the interpretation of what our potential customers actually need than "voice of the customer" or "customer mind reader" would imply. The best way I can describe this is that we read between the lines of our market's narrative. We appreciate and understand the meaning behind what people do tell us, and we appreciate the lacunae—the details people omit—as well. And unlike the priests who translated the Pythia's crazed pronouncements into ambiguous advice, we need to be as clear and specific as possible when we provide guidance on the future direction of our products.

The truth is that a product manager is no oracle—the fate of any product is always something of a mystery. Even the most successful companies call it wrong every now and again. Conducting lots of market research early on may not predict the future precisely, but common sense would dictate that doing so would improve your product's chances of success over pure guesswork. You'd also expect that companies would learn from earlier mistakes, and yet, as George Santayana writes in his book *The Life of Reason*:

> Progress, far from consisting in change, depends on retentiveness. When change is absolute there remains no being to improve and no direction is set for possible improvement: and when experience is not retained, as among savages, infancy is perpetual. Those who cannot remember the past are condemned to repeat it.[29]

With some commentators observing that we may be in the midst of another tech bubble, we're reminded of how much clearer the causes of product failure appear in hindsight. Might one undoubtedly brilliant company be about to see another Segway-sized failure? For fun, let's compare Segway with Google Glass:

Segway: 2001	Glass: 2013
Great engineering	Great engineering
Created in a tech bubble	Created in a tech bubble
Massively hyped before launch	Massively hyped before launch
For the tech-savvy, by the tech-savvy	For the tech-savvy, by the tech-savvy
Illegal to use when most likely to be of use	Illegal to use when most likely to be of use[30]
Mainstream users feel a bit daft using it	Mainstream users feel a bit daft using it
A solution in search of a problem	A solution in search of a problem*

* If I need to pull up information from the Internet while I'm walking down a crowded street, I already can do so on my smartphone, and I don't have to shout to myself to make it work.

Plus ça change, plus c'est la même chose—the more things change, the more they stay the same. Of course Glass may become the new iPhone. The uncertainty is what makes product management so continually challenging.

The best we can do to solve the mystery of whether a product will succeed or fail is to coax out the truth from what our users do and don't say. This is why the role of the product manager deserves more than a facile label. It's one thing to be the voice of the customer; it's an entirely more valuable skill to understand what the customer is saying.

POINTS TO REMEMBER

Knowing the Customers Better Than They Know Themselves

» People rarely know their own minds, so your challenge is to read between the lines to distinguish between what they think they want and what they really need.

» Get out there and check your assumptions, particularly the most risky ones—you don't want to "do a Segway."

» A gap in the market may exist for a good reason. Make sure there is a market in the gap of real people with a pervasive, urgent, and valuable problem they can't easily solve for themselves, but which you can solve for them, profitably.

» People need a strong motivation to buy a product. Ask yourself, "What's in it for them?"

» The value of a product varies according to how much it's needed, and people's needs change over time. Time your request for payment with when your product is needed most.

» Real-world benefits, not features, sell products. Ask yourself, "So what?"

» Be creative to run quick, cheap, and easy tests to check your assumptions. Always be learning.

» When describing your typical users, paint pictures in the mind by telling a memorable and relevant story about them.

Chapter 3

YOU'RE ACTUALLY MANAGING PEOPLE, NOT PRODUCTS

I hope by this point you've begun to feel a sense of enthusiasm about product management and understand why it's so important and how stimulating and rewarding the work is. There is excitement in the journey of bringing a new product to life. But the job isn't for everyone, and this is in large part because it involves not only managing products, but managing people.

Product managers will almost always both report to a manager and manage other people. You're responsible for the collective efforts of a virtual team of people across the different departments within your company, even though none of them report directly to you. And if all goes well, at some point you'll probably also end up directly managing other product managers, as well as business analysts and possibly even developers and designers. Your product's success (and so your own) is largely contingent on your ability to understand, relate to, and influence others well. One of the side effects of being hooked into so many different aspects of your organization is that you'll quickly uncover the dysfunction. Every company has some kind of dysfunction—whether a charming eccentricity or a less desirable habit—so you just have to figure out how to cope with the various kinds of dysfunctional behavior. And that can get rocky.

As the one in the center of the three rings, the product manager bears much of the burden of reconciling competing views and goals. The most common ways in which any organization goes wrong boil down to the triumvirate of poor communication, incompetent or adversarial senior managers (those with a "them and us" mindset), and lack of alignment with a shared vision. These are all people problems—and you're the person in the eye of the storm who has to overcome them. I'll be honest, the job can sometimes feel like a struggle against the machinations of people whose sole purpose in life is to derail your product at every turn. Jean-Paul Sartre wrote in his play *No Exit*, "Hell is other people." On some days, I know exactly what he means.

A product manager is often described as the "CEO of the product," but this is misleading—you will rarely have any of the direct authority that the term *CEO* implies over other departments, and sometimes only limited authority over the development team. This is why you've got to achieve success almost entirely through influencing others to follow your plan, which is made much more challenging by the fact that more often than not your coworkers fail to understand your role or appreciate your value. To have the necessary influence, you must empathize with all the various players, speak their language, and earn their respect. The good news is that the sorts of issues that come up tend to fall into categories with which you become familiar, and you will get better and better at heading them off at the pass.

Every new product assignment is an exploration into treacherous terrain, and like a clumsy explorer, over the years I've tripped into every ravine, poked every wild bear with a stick, and been bitten by every poisonous snake. Along the way I learned to have a good deal of humility, and I tell my Golden Rule—to ignore or do the opposite of what I suggest—to every product team I work with. The advantage of my mistakes is that I've learned some valuable things about how to work most effectively with each of the main groups of people you'll be working with as a product manager. Here I want to give you a sense of what their respective roles *should* be when done well, and also illustrate the typical dysfunctions that crop up and how you might circumnavigate them. Are there organizations out there that have only paragons of excellence working for them? Absolutely. Have I bumped into any of them? *Occasionally.* Most often, you'll have one or another laggard or difficult person to cope with.

I should also hasten to add that although I have performed each of the following roles in at least a basic capacity at some point in my career, which I hope qualifies me to make some observations from both sides of the fence, I make no claim to be an expert in any. I should also mention again that my experience has been almost exclusively in creating software products, so the personnel and issues covered are specific to that domain. But the issues that come up are mostly fundamental human issues, so they are likely quite similar in any product domain.

THE DEVELOPMENT TEAM

A product manager's relationship with the development (or engineering) team is one of the most important ones to get right, so I'll start with them. Software developers are an interesting bunch, but they can often be a difficult group of people to work with, particularly if you don't come from a technical background yourself. Google, as mentioned earlier, only recruits product managers with computer science backgrounds, on the basis that anyone less technical will fail to "earn the respect of the engineering team."[1] Developers' impatience with a lack of technical knowledge is perfectly understandable; to them programming languages, frameworks, software architecture, operating systems, networks, and the workings of hardware are the stuff of daily nuts-and-bolts process. Each comes with its own sets of rules and constraints, and a developer has to negotiate all those constraints like a multidimensional crossword puzzle in order to make the product actually work. Unaware and unrealistic designs can be infuriating.

The really good developers can instinctively tell from a set of your software requirements where the complexity, performance bottlenecks, and other difficulties will arise in making the vision a reality. And that's before they encounter a previously undiscovered bug in one of the many different building blocks of third-party software they're relying on to assemble what you need, which necessitates them to either rethink the whole approach or undertake a massive development detour to work around the problem. They're like car mechanics who can diagnose a leaking cylinder head gasket from the sound of a running engine alone and can strip down and fix the offending part by the end of the afternoon—but more so. Developers are miracle workers. They turn a product vision into reality and make it look easy.

If you really want to annoy development, follow these easy steps:

>> Have no technical understanding whatsoever, nor any desire to acquire it.
>> Be vague or ambiguous in your product requirements.
>> Belittle tasks by declaring that they can't be that hard.
>> Never use the product.
>> Change your mind without warning and then expect delivery timescales to remain the same.
>> Shift all blame for a product disaster to the development team.
>> Shout and stamp your feet like a child when you really want things done.
>> Never provide context or reasoning for any decision.
>> Start offering advice on how to implement a feature, even though you have no idea how to do so.
>> Use technical terms you don't know the meaning of.*
>> Never consult the opinion of anyone in development before making a technical decision.

---

* Bonus step: be ungrammatical and finish sentences with a preposition.

» Promise features to customers or the board without first checking whether they're possible.

» Never celebrate releases or customer wins with the development team.

If, on the other hand, you want to work well with them, develop a good understanding of the difficulties they're dealing with, which many people at most companies neglect to do.

Your relationship with the developers is important for many reasons, but one is that very often the senior management regards the development team as obstructive and slow-moving. Of course, occasionally the criticism is justified, but more often than not the development team is perfectly capable and senior management has unreasonable expectations of how much can be achieved in a given period of time, or the product has become so knotted up that even a simple change takes ages. The team's efficiency may also be hamstrung by a collection of outmoded, complex procedures that they're obliged to follow but have no authority to streamline, which upper management tends not to want to hear about.

Of course there's no denying that developers can sometimes be hard to work with. People with minds finely attuned to the nuances and complex interactions of software can have a tendency to relish minutiae over the big picture—sometimes to an obsessive degree. When coupled with an almost religious fervor for the "right" way to do things and a surprisingly vigorous approach to arguing their point when someone suggests any alternative path, they can be incredibly frustrating people.

Early in my career, when I was still working as a tech support operative at Zeus Technology, I could always easily provoke the entire development team into a heated debate. I'd just lob a conversational hand grenade into their midst, such as asking which of the two predominant text editors at the time was better for writing code. Developers can also be undeniably geeky. I remember one Zeus social evening where at one end of the room the sales guys were belting out songs on the karaoke machine, spilling their pints of beer, while at the other end the development team had rigged up a multiplayer computer game and were all huddled around a table, glued to their monitors.

In any team of people you'll find a spread of personalities, and developers are no different. I've found, though, that they do tend to break down into types: the visionary, most likely scribbling frenetically on a whiteboard somewhere, possibly while wearing a hat and cloak; the deep but narrow-range specialist, often a sage-like character whom the more junior developers are slightly scared of; the perfectionist, who's most likely to be engaged in a pedantic argument over an inconsequential aspect of programming; and the no-fuss, get-it-done implementer. You'll hopefully also find among them the team player, an immensely useful inside man who can defuse arguments and mediate with the rest of the team to come to consensus on which way is in fact the "right" way.

I'll be the first to admit that personality foibles go both ways. The developers I've had the pleasure of working with have also had to put up with my early-morning cognitive failures and occasional grumpiness. And it has to be said that product managers can step outside their expertise and make the mistake of micromanaging development. There have been many occasions when I've strayed too far from specifying what we need and why, and into *how* I want it to be delivered. And if you've ever been told how to do your job by someone who only vaguely understands what you do, then you'll appreciate how immensely annoying that can be.

When it comes down to it, most developers share a desire to work on interesting, stimulating projects and to be recognized in the way they would like for their good work, just like every other person. Keeping this squarely in mind in your interactions with them will go a long way toward helping you cope with the irritations. Try to become sympathetic to the many sources of their own frustrations.

One development team I worked with was still largely Waterfall in approach and prioritized features by the MoSCoW method, which is short for *Must* have, *Should* have, *Could* have, and *Would* (or *Won't*) have. Their quality control procedures required them to provide time and effort estimates for all items designated as Musts and Shoulds, and I've yet to meet a developer who enjoyed creating estimates. In the context of a large organization that was trying to manage the availability of a limited number of developers across multiple projects competing for their time, this seemed to management to be a sensible approach, but in practice the process of estimation often took as long (or longer) than it would have taken to just fix the problem there and then.

So on one project, in which we were primarily going to be squashing software bugs, I turned to my assembled developers and suggested conspiratorially that I would make every single product requirement a Could, providing they agreed to work from the top of the priorities list downward in order until they ran out of time. This meant they didn't need to waste their time on creating estimates that were bound to be wrong, and instead could concentrate on fixing bugs, which they did in quantity. Everyone was happy except for the senior development managers, who were a bit miffed that we had subverted their lovely quality control process. But the team got the job done. Sometimes developers are just looking for permission to operate in another way because they've been micromanaged into inefficiency.

Developers also like to be free to exercise their creativity, which can lead to great things. However, creativity can be a double-edged sword. While a bit of lateral thinking can neatly sidestep an obstacle, it may also lead a project off track. So though you don't want to second-guess their every move, if your team is stumped by a particular problem, you should work through the obstacles with them. One thing I've learned to do in that event is to get them to explain their assumptions. You may find that they're working hard to preserve the function of something in your product that is no longer very important, and once it's taken out of the equation, the way forward is much simpler for the developers. Again, it can boil down to the rules they feel compelled to follow; if you've previously told them not to break existing product features, then they'll do their utmost to respect your wishes. You just need to remember to tell them when they're allowed to make an exception.

In some cases, creativity can also lead to a "science project" where a left-field, convoluted approach is chosen over a more straightforward choice because it's cool or difficult or has never been done before or will demonstrate the developers' Jedi prowess. This can result in tech for tech's sake, and developers sometimes need to be reminded that the fact they *can* do something doesn't mean they *should*. Always keep an eye out for science projects—if the proposed solution seems overly complex, get a second opinion and rein things in.

Developers can be wary of people in suits who tend to disrupt the development team's peace and routine with unreasonable and unexpected requests. Product managers may occasionally have to wear suits, but you should really try to avoid being categorized by development as *a suit*. It's very easy for your developers to perceive you as just another disturbance that's going to make their lives more difficult for a while, lose interest or fail, and then go away. So for them, ignoring you can be an effective strategy. Particularly if you're new to the company, you may have to work quite hard to disabuse them of this impression. You need to become a black-belt expert on your product, its quirks, and its undocumented features (read: bugs) and penetrate the obfuscating technical jargon that may be keeping you from understanding things fully. Only at that point will you be able to prove your worth to the development team and earn their respect. Once you get there, the benefits of a working relationship based on mutual respect are boundless.

THE DESIGN DUO

Design is a mystical art to me. I appreciate good design when I see and feel it, but I'm simply not wired to do it well myself, a fact readily apparent to anyone who's seen one of my homebrew presentations—they're so garish they can induce seizures even from a distance. So to me, a good designer is a magician who can conjure into my mind the instant understanding of what a product is and how it should be used, and I'm always slightly in awe of those who can do this. (Just keep that between you and me.)

In working with designers it helps to appreciate that they tend to be schooled in design principles, which generally matter a good deal to them. One of those principles that I've come to appreciate in the same way is the mandate for simplicity. Aziz Musa is an all-around product good guy who delivered a fantastic talk at the Mind the Product conference in London in 2013 on what he calls "pure products."[2] A pure product is one that combines profound simplicity with beauty. Musa explains that "profound simplicity is not merely the *absence* of complexity, it is the exquisite *mastery* of it." A product that has been stripped down to a single capability is *superficially* simple because it can do only one thing, whereas a product that remains simple to use despite its inherent complexity is *profoundly* simple. Think of those old Palm Pilot personal digital assistants that only really had a calendar, a to-do list, and an address book (superficially simple) in comparison with an iPhone that is a communication device, a camera, a portal to the Internet, and a library of your entire music and book collection and yet remains simple enough to use without recourse to a thousand-page instruction manual. And it happens to have apps that provide a calendar, a to-do list, and an address book. That's profound simplicity.

Beauty, Musa continues poetically, is a matter of more than just aesthetics; it's that indefinable stirring in one's soul on seeing something truly beautiful. Shakespeare eloquently describes the same feeling in Ferdinand's speech to Miranda in *The Tempest*:

> ...*Hear my soul speak:*
> *The very instant that I saw you, did*
> *My heart fly to your service; there resides,*
> *To make me slave to it*[3]

Good designers can take the complex and make it profoundly simple. Great designers will also stir your soul and bewitch you with the beauty of their design.

But like developers, designers can be difficult, and again, they come in several flavors. You'll be most likely to encounter a particular design duo. The first half is on the more creative range of the spectrum. Visual (or graphic) designers create all sorts of hard-to-discern items, such as mood boards, and gather other eclectic and eccentric sources of inspiration that may seem alien if, like me, you don't have a visually creative bone in your body. Visual designers combine psychology and symbolism with colors and imagery to evoke the desired feelings with their designs. Give them some time and space and you'll be astonished by what they create. It may not be remotely practical, but it will probably be beautiful.

At this point you can start to bring to bear some of your user-centric, analytical thinking, which you should do with a good dollop of tact. The initial visual designs may turn out to be bat-shit crazy, but there's usually a kernel of brilliance in there somewhere that will resonate with the user. Acknowledge and appreciate the designers' creation, but then work with them to focus and iterate on the part that's relevant. There's always a temptation to get swept up in the process of creating beautiful things and digress off the track of combining form *and* function. If you work with designers in a spirit of appreciation, they will usually value that you're keeping at least one foot on the ground for them.

User experience (UX) or interaction designers are the other part of the duo, and they're a somewhat different breed. While the visual designers are the ones creating snapshots of particular aspects of the product to illustrate the colors, typography, iconography, and layout, the interaction designers are the ones who detail how users move from one snapshot to another in practice. UX designers also bring consistency, the intelligible system of visual clues that users need in order to understand how to use the product. These people should be some of your greatest allies, as they, like you, are meant to focus on the needs of the users and the ways in which those users experience the product. UX designers take the product's purpose (to allow a user to complete one or more specific tasks) and design the ways in which the product will help the users achieve their goals.

In interacting with UX people, I've generally found that they're largely in sync with product managers, but there are some pitfalls to watch out for. One is that UX designers may want more time to do user research, build prototypes, and test the product than the development budget allows for. They may want to add some features, like cool new interfaces, that you don't have the time or budget for the developers to program. You may also clash with them regarding what's really in the users' best interests. For one thing, UX designers are specialists in determining that, so they may claim bragging rights. But as with developers, there is always a danger that UX designers will fall back to designing for themselves rather than the target user. The research you yourself have done about users will help avoid this and provide a basis for discussing user issues in the UX designers' own terms. Take the time to come to agreement about the user personas, which UX designers also work with, and to carefully consider any user research they've conducted. You may well be failing to appreciate the ways in which the design they're proposing really will enhance the users' appreciation of the product.

One of the most important ways in which you'll be working with the design duo is by adjudicating between them and the front-end developers, who take the largely theoretical or mocked-up work of designers and render it as a working interface. The practicalities of implementing a design in code will sometimes necessitate compromise in the designs, and this is where you can be especially helpful in smoothing things out. Most visual designers still come from a print media background, which is arguably more forgiving than digital media these days. In print, a designer had to think about a relatively small number of possible levels of detail, whereas in the digital world, he has to take into account the various resolutions and screen sizes of all the different devices available, ranging from the smallest smartphone display; to desktop monitors of varying age, size, and clarity; through to the intensely high-resolution displays sported by the Apple-endowed. In print, designers never had to worry about pixel alignment to ensure their designs were clearly rendered or contend with readers attempting to resize the page. This gulf in complexity between print and digital design is one reason there can be clashes between designers and the developers.

A welcome trend that may circumvent this disconnect is the emergence of hybrid front-end developer-designers. Ordinarily a developer who claimed to be a front-end designer would be deluding himself. Just sneak a look at the screen of your local coffee shop next time you visit. The blocky, Windows-looking software styled from circa 1997 running on the point-of-sale device may be functional, but it sure ain't pretty. And I'll bet the baristas' souls don't exactly sing when they use it, either. However, there is an increasing number of developers who have legitimate design credentials as well as the technical know-how to write code. Hopefully there will be many more of them in the coming years.

MARKETING MAGIC AND MAYHEM

In many aspects, marketing and product management are similar; you could even say they're codependent. Both involve two-way conversations with the market to understand its demography and needs and to make the people in your target niche aware that there is now a valuable solution to their specific problems. The research that marketing undertakes and distills should be of immense value to you as input into the creation and direction of products. Similarly, their specialist understanding of the most effective ways to communicate information back to the target market, in terms of channels, media, content, voice, and tone, should ensure that the hard work that's gone into the product is not wasted because your organization is unable to tell anyone about it effectively. In addition, if you're working in a business-to-consumer (B2C) company, you'll be less likely to have an in-house sales team, so you'll probably be selling direct through your own website, a marketplace, or an affiliate network, in which case the "selling" comes from the effectiveness of your advertising, search engine optimization (SEO), and product copy—all of which are the domain of your marketing team.

Then there's the care with which marketing manages the brand, both of the company and the product (as the two may have distinct brand identities). Brand identity can be an immensely powerful asset as, over time, it becomes a shorthand for a desirable collection of qualities and feelings that customers associate with the company or product. As Wally Olins, the late, great chairman of Saffron Brand Consultants, put it:

> A brand is about having a unique idea, personality and style and demonstrating it in everything that you do, in your products, in the way your people behave, in your communications, advertising and other promotions, and in your environments, your offices and showrooms. A brand is not a logo, it's a presentation of who you are and what you stand for in everything you do and to every audience with whom you deal.[4]

When you think of Rolls-Royce cars, you perhaps think of British refinement, elegance, and opulence. When you think of Volvo, you probably think of solid build quality, middle age, and passenger safety (and probably not raciness). But brand perception is another double-edged sword. Negative associations with a brand can be extremely difficult to change. Take the case of luxury electric-vehicle manufacturer Tesla Motors, which had to fight a PR rearguard action after the press published photos in 2013 of Tesla's cars on fire at the side of the road.[5]

A good marketing team can be just as magical as a talented design team, but marketing people can also sometimes be vexing. Market research, communication, and brand management are all specialist disciplines intrinsic to the success of a product, yet some of the marketers I've worked with failed to understand the importance of developing expertise in these disciplines. In fairness, some were saddled with having to market a lackluster product that hadn't changed significantly since the previous millennium in a fiercely competitive market. Despite their best efforts, they were never going to achieve great success. But time and again in different companies I see the same dysfunctions cropping up.

At Zeus Technology, marketing's solution to seemingly every problem was an expensive yet extremely subtle "rebrand"—by which they actually meant just changing the logo colors and fonts. Looking back at the archives of the website, I counted at least seven logo changes in ten years. For a while, the logo was changing every year. The design agencies must have been laughing into their Pantone mugs when they heard us coming.

On other occasions, style would overtake substance (and common sense). During a recruitment campaign, the marketing team seized upon the idea of enticing individual candidates with the message: "We won't keep your brain in a box." So they mailed out white twenty-inch-square presentation boxes (which looked like they should contain luxury chocolates), each with a shelled walnut half glued to the center. The walnut was meant to resemble a small brain. And apart from the slightly mixed message of not wanting to keep, and yet actively presenting, brains in a box, the impact was further undermined: first, there was the note enclosed saying the glued-in walnut shouldn't be eaten for health reasons; second, because marketing had failed to apply the correct postage, the lucky recipient had to pay for the privilege of receiving a massive box containing an inedible nut resembling a mouse brain, all as an enticement to join a forward-thinking software startup.

Another dysfunction occurs when marketers believe that *market research* means exclusively *focus groups* and parrot back every sound bite from a focus group as the gospel truth without delving any deeper into the findings. "Eight out of ten customers we interviewed said our products were too expensive, so we need to reduce our prices." With qualitative feedback such as this, it may in fact be the case that the products are overpriced; however, it's equally possible that customers are not realizing the full benefits or value of the product, or that the product is not suited to the market segment targeted (and hence is not valued), or that the canny customers are simply angling for a discount. It could even be that the interviewer inadvertently introduced bias when conducting the research with a leading question: "Do you think our products are expensive?" Without further research into the product's value and pricing within its intended market niche, it's not possible to say for sure whether products are overpriced.

A good deal of research has shown that focus groups can lead to mistaken conclusions. One glaring example is that of the focus group response to a new sneaker design Reebok was considering. As Gianfranco Zaccai, founder and president of Continuum, the design group that devised the sneaker concept, recalls:

> When Continuum pitched an idea to Reebok for a new basketball shoe that would use inflated air to better support the ankle, thereby reducing injuries, the brand manager for basketball shoes said he wasn't interested because he had never heard about a need for that from a focus group. When we proposed the idea to a high school basketball team, the response was even worse—the players openly laughed at the concept.
>
> But when the team members actually used an early "experiential model" of the shoe during practice, they were won over by how cool it was to have a shoe form-fitted to their feet. Over time, they were even more enthusiastic as they realized they could play more confidently without fear of injury. Like that, the Reebok Pump was born.[6]

Marketing teams may favor qualitative market research because it's relatively easy to conduct and seems to yield useful results. However, interviews and focus groups are also susceptible to various research biases, particularly moderator acceptance bias (interviewees may try to give the answer they think the interviewer is looking for rather than an honest response) and sensitivity bias (focus group participants may not wish to admit weakness or a personal failing in front of their peers). I've found that these two biases crop up particularly often in usability tests, themselves a form of qualitative research.

In 2013, I was moderating some usability tests on a data visualization prototype in Rwanda with government employees. In that country, at least in the ten or so government departments I visited, there was a very strong management hierarchy. Employees showed great deference and respect to their managers, to the extent that their desire to impress their bosses (and outshine their peers) clearly biased their behavior and responses. For this reason, to allow the interviewee to feel comfortable enough to make "mistakes" in the usability test and give honest feedback, I had to ensure that I ran the tests strictly on a one-on-one basis (a good idea generally), meaning that I'd sometimes have to shoo the interviewee's manager and colleagues politely but firmly from the room.

Similarly, a dominant voice on a focus group panel may cause other participants to follow the leader (dominant respondent bias), or in other situations a herd mentality may emerge (social acceptance bias). As an illustration of these peer-driven effects, Tom Webster from Edison Research described how researchers at the University of Glasgow once observed different results depending on whether individual interviews were conducted before or after focus groups:

In 1994, Daniel Wight, a senior researcher at the University of Glasgow, studied the opinions of adolescent boys as they relate to the opposite sex. In individual interviews, the boys expressed sensitive, sympathetic portraits of their opinions on girls, while in subsequent focus groups their opinions exhibited considerably more "machismo." In contrast, a second group began with focus groups first, again expressing fairly chauvinistic views, and ended with individual interviews, in which they maintained the macho views expressed in the focus groups.[7]

On the positive side, it's good that some companies are at least going out to listen to their markets, but as we explored in the previous chapter, customers can be unaware of some of their most important needs, so they're not necessarily going to be able to articulate them in a one-on-one interview or focus group. To use the clichéd quote attributed to economist Theodore Levitt, "People don't want to buy a quarter-inch drill, they want a quarter-inch hole." Also, relying solely on these qualitative techniques for market research will at best provide only general insight. This may allow researchers to form a hunch (or hypothesis) of where the market has an unmet need, but it will not provide enough detail to allow them to really home in on how the product should meet that need. This is why it's still necessary to supplement the qualitative research with quantitative testing, using the Kano method introduced in the previous chapter or other data-driven techniques. Simply parroting back what the market says it wants verbatim, without reading between the lines, will rarely uncover latent needs.

A particular bugbear I have with some marketing people is that they are seemingly incapable of communicating without jargon. Strangely, for a group of people whose role necessitates frequent communication with their market, it is too often the case that they fail to communicate clearly. B2B companies seem to be particularly susceptible. Surely not all business products need to be described as "leveraging synergies" between one thing and another, or "lowering the total cost of ownership." My theory is that marketing people who resort to this nonsense are simply throwing up a smokescreen, whether consciously or not, to obscure the fact that they have failed to grasp what the product is, what it does, and how it benefits customers in their target market.

Sometimes this lack of knowledge is readily apparent. There was a startup called Splashpower operating out of the office next to ours when I was at Zeus that was a pioneer in wireless charging pads that would recharge the batteries of mobile phones and similar devices placed upon them. In a possibly unwise move, without consulting the engineering team, its marketing team boldly claimed that the company would soon be able to produce a room-sized charging pad that could charge devices while they were still in people's pockets. Had they bothered to check with engineering first, they'd have established that a charging device of this size and power would essentially micro-wave the occupants of the room.

Another pitfall is that marketing teams sometimes end up at the beck and call of the sales team and are pigeonholed into spending all their time generating ever-increasing numbers of customer leads for sales to pursue. This can be a particularly pernicious setup, because the fact that the sales team has delegated (read: shrugged off) respon-sibility for finding their business opportunities may indicate that they don't understand the product or target market (or perhaps are just too lazy). Marketing teams are often given a corresponding finan-cial or conversion rate target on the leads they generate. This would be reasonable if the sales team could be relied on to sell the product competently, but it's tricky if sales doesn't understand the product and market. Meanwhile, the marketing team is likely neglecting other valuable parts of their job.

Whether because the sales team's conversion rate of leads to sales is dropping or there is a revenue shortfall in a particular month or quarter, the poor performance of sales may result in the marketing team being forced to run more and more knee-jerk campaigns to an increasingly irritated market base. In other words, sheer demand for sales leads will sacrifice quality of marketing for quantity. Instead, it might be more prudent in this situation to examine the underlying causes of the dropping conversion rate. It could be the result of poor quality of leads in the first place, the inability of the sales team to convert the high-quality leads they're being fed, a mixture of both, or something else entirely. Rather than simply generating more low-quality leads, a more considered marketing approach would be to take a step back and identify who in the target market would be more likely to need the product and how best to let them know the product exists.

This is where you, the product manager, come in. In the previous chapter, we looked at how important it is for you to step into the shoes of your target market and understand the needs and pains of the vari-ous user personas you define. Whether you're gathering this market research single-handedly or with the assistance of dedicated market researchers, you should be involved firsthand. Your goal should be to involve the marketing team and share with them as much of this valuable research as possible. This will help them keep their sights on the needs of the market rather than the needs of the sales team. By highlighting to marketing the segments that you anticipate will be more interested in certain products or features over others and explaining how and why the product features solve the users' problems, you will help them communicate effectively with each segment. Even if your product is complex or technical, you should always be able to explain or demonstrate its concept simply and succinctly to nonexperts, and by helping marketing do so as well, you will forge a strong relationship and reduce the potential for counterproductive clashes.

HARD SALES

Many business-to-consumer (B2C) software products are sold directly to customers from a website or app store, but you may also work for a company with a dedicated sales team such as Oracle, SAP, or IBM that sells enterprise products like database systems and supply chain software. If you're managing these kinds of business-to-business (B2B) products, you'll probably be dealing quite a bit with the sales group. Times are changing, however, and more B2B companies are now selling their products directly, like B2C products. Take FreeAgent, an accounting web application, for example, and MailChimp's success in offering self-service email marketing.

If you do work with a sales team, you're likely to find that salespeople are by nature shy, retiring types who need constant reassurance. Well, not quite. Salespeople generally work on a commission basis, and, frankly, this can make them somewhat loony. Some of them are so aggressive they probably found the movies *Glengarry Glen Ross* and *Wall Street* to be instructive guides rather than cautionary tales. Salespeople can annoy customers by constantly pressuring them to buy, so much so that customers may resort in desperation to buying something they don't really want on the off chance that the salesperson might then leave them alone. That is not exactly what we'd call a healthy customer relationship.

It's part of the natural order of things that salespeople will want product management and marketing to create every conceivable product document, crib sheet, presentation, one-pager, and demo *but will never read them*. It seems with some salespeople that on the day they join the company, they learn some patter to describe what the product does, probably from an equally ill-informed colleague, and keep using it for years, regardless of how much the product changes.

There are, of course, some great salespeople, and the best of them can be an important source of customer feedback and product ideas. But there's no denying that others are boors, have undergone a dual empathy and common sense bypass, or are genuinely lovely people but lack the pushiness to close deals well. As a product manager, you're going to have to learn to cope with both good and bad salespeople if you want your product to be successful in the long run. So here's a quick guide to the fine art of sales team relations.

There are three broad types of bad salespeople: demanders, strugglers, and inventors. Demanders will not take no for an answer. One of the product managers on my team once told a particular sales guy—let's call him Todd—that he wasn't permitted to sell a product to a customer because it was sensitive, highly regulated, and was to be sold only to government agencies. Shortly afterward, Todd's manager turned up to harangue me with a line that may become familiar to you: *"Why is your team standing in the way of my sales team? They pay your salary."* After pointing out that selling the product in question would mean the managing director would go to jail for breach of the UK's Data Protection Act, I left him to consider his next move while I went to make tea.

In contrast with the overt aggression of demanders, strugglers feign ineptitude to attract people's sympathy and appeal to their helpful nature. Strugglers turn up at customer meetings and ask to borrow pens and paper from the client because they forgot to bring any themselves, or ask you to help them with a customer demo "because you're *so good* at it." Before you know it, you've pitched the product, overcome the customer's objections, and closed the deal for the salesperson, leaving him to rake in the commission while you wonder what the hell just happened.

Then you've got the inventors, the ones who take two or more unrelated products, amalgamate them into a single (nonexistent) entity during a customer pitch, and sell their new "creation." Then they blame you when you break the news to them that not only does this chimera product not exist (surprise, surprise), but the two legitimate products don't play nicely with each other, and getting them to do so would cost several times more than they've sold the invented one for. That's the product's fault, they contend, so it should be the product manager's problem to fix.

I'll be the first to admit that sales makes an easy target for product managers and that deep down, we quite enjoy having a token bad guy to be exasperated by, particularly when we're venting over a post-work beverage. Salespeople can drive you crazy, but just remember that in B2B companies they are primarily responsible for getting your product out there and that they have the stamina to do the hard selling that we would not enjoy. For every customer who says yes and buys, the salesperson has had to brazen out twenty or more rejections. Salespeople live by the sword and die by the sword, with generally low basic salaries and most of their income from commission. The system is set up for them to do everything they can to make deals.

So in working with them, put yourself in their shoes. Try to forgive them for being a little caught up in where their next commission check is coming from. Think about how you could demonstrate to them that their success rate will improve if they listen to what you're saying. Work to understand their selling process and find ways to supply them with the product information they need, when they need it and in a form they can use more easily and quickly. I quite liked one enterprising product manager's approach of having drink coasters printed with some product sound bites and leaving them on the telesales team's desks. Another approach I've seen work well was to encourage an underperforming sales team to attend short (less than an hour) workshops with their peers and the product manager. When we opened up the challenges to the group, the more successful salespeople would share their tips because they loved to talk about their own successes, and the rest would be more likely to take advice from peers than from product managers.

It can be tempting to think that you can sell the product better than sales, so I recommend that you have a try. You may be shocked—selling is *hard*. Always keep that in mind when dealing with salespeople.

MANAGING UP

Until you're running your own company, you'll always be reporting up to someone. Unless, that is, you work for one of the few firms that have tossed out hierarchical management. Valve, the software company behind ridiculously successful game titles such as the *Half-Life* and *Portal* series, defies convention by having an entirely flat organizational structure, which will have you either reaching for your résumé or recoiling in horror at the apparent anarchy of it all. Valve's employee handbook states:

> Hierarchy is great for maintaining predictability and repeatability.... We want innovators, and that means maintaining an environment where they'll flourish. That's why Valve is flat. It's our shorthand way of saying that we don't have any management, and nobody "reports to" anybody else. We do have a founder/president, but even he isn't your manager. This company is yours to steer—toward opportunities and away from risks. You have the power to green-light projects. You have the power to ship products.[8]

I think it's safe to say that this style of management will take a long time to catch on widely, if it ever does. Most of us are going to have a higher-up, and if you're lucky, that person will be someone who understands what your role is; leaves you to get on with it; supports you when you need support; occasionally runs interference for you; and diplomatically steps in from time to time in order to nudge you in the right direction, allowing you to fulfill your professional potential. If you're really unlucky, you could end up with an incompetent cretin who's only looking out for number one and whose very presence stifles team productivity and reduces morale. Your manager will sit somewhere along the spectrum between these two extremes, though hopefully toward the more supportive end. And bear in mind that those you must manage up to include other corporate higher-ups in addition to your immediate boss, such as the heads of sales and marketing and the CEO.

When dealing with higher-ups, always think about their needs and challenges; they're probably time-poor and have several other concerns competing for their attention. Fundamentally, they need to understand from you whether you're handling everything satisfactorily or whether they need to intervene. Consider the relative importance of your product in the context of everything else that's going on. If your product accounts for 75 percent of all company revenue, and it has a problem that may adversely affect that revenue, it's probably worth bringing the problem (and some ideas to solve it) to the attention of the management, starting with your boss. Highlighting how many bugs you fixed in the latest incremental update probably shouldn't be treated as front-page news.

As you would when thinking about your user personas, assess how each of your higher-ups prefers to give and receive information and tailor your approach accordingly. Say the head of sales gives you a regular slot to present at the monthly sales meeting: Keep it brief and enthuse them. Always be clear and as definite as possible, but never be afraid to say you don't know something. Just make certain you know the answer for next time. As many professional storytellers recommend, when presenting, show, don't tell. Illustrate the point you're trying to make as engagingly as you can, whether it's by showing video excerpts from user tests highlighting the problem you need the funding to fix or by demonstrating a prototype that shows succinctly how you've successfully solved a problem in the product. When you're finished, you may also wish to leave a summary or some further reading for people to review at their leisure. (I suggest not giving it to them at the start, as then they will be paying attention to it rather than you.) Enliven any hard statistics with infographics that make the point clear at a glance. Be sensitive to what Nobel Prize–winning economist and psychologist Daniel Kahneman calls cognitive ease (literally making text easier to read by improving its visual contrast). You always want to use the simplest, most direct visuals and language you can. Keep in mind a finding by UCLA professor Danny Oppenheimer that Kahneman writes about in his book *Thinking, Fast and Slow*. Oppenheimer found that using unnecessarily obscure or complex words actually reduces credibility and is considered a sign of low intelligence.

Despite the stereotypes, managers are rarely simpletons, but if they're only going to give you their undivided attention for five minutes a month, make it memorable and easy for them to consume the information. You want to instill in them the sense that you're in control and are a safe pair of hands. If you do so, you'll become someone they'll really listen to, and they'll look forward to hearing from you, even if the news isn't always good. After all, you never know when you might need to take advantage of their goodwill for a favor.

When I joined Experian in 2008, the routine in our business unit was that the product team had to request any significant budget needed to work on our products, and this request required a business case. And like the development estimates on which they were based, our business cases were typically wrong, regardless of how much effort we expended researching and creating them. There were simply too many assumptions and variable elements all stacked up on each other. Nevertheless, no business case meant no funding, so we knuckled down and did the best we could to predict the future. Our problem was that each business case took someone two to three weeks to pull together, yet most were rejected by senior management. This was a colossal waste of time for all concerned, so we attempted to improve the process.

What we came up with was a one-slide, five-minute pitch with the single goal of determining from the management team as quickly as possible whether it was worth devoting the time to a full-fledged business case. The pitch answered the following questions about the proposed product or feature: What is it? Who's it for? And what's it worth? We made no attempt to speculate how much the development would cost, as we didn't yet know, and we'd cram three or four pitches, including taking questions, into each month's time slot. The ideas were either shelved, given the go-ahead for a full-blown business case, or in some cases green-lighted for immediate delivery there and then. This approach had three effects: First, the "lightning pitch" aspect was lively and far more engaging. Our product pitches actually became a welcome diversion for the management from their normal agenda. Second, we saved lots of time by pushing for an early decision on whether to pursue or ditch each idea by weeding out the ones that would never have been approved. Third, we could use the time we saved to generate, research, and propose more ideas than before, allowing us to be more innovative.

MANAGING DOWN

If you've ever worked for a boss who was a micromanager or a seagull—one that swoops in unexpectedly, makes a whole bunch of noise, and craps on everybody—you'll know the experience is not pleasant. Try very hard to avoid adopting these management styles. My own first attempt at line management was an abject failure. Very early in my working career at Zeus, the company was growing so rapidly that pretty much everyone was able to recruit an underling. Despite being just the guy responsible for the websites at the time, I somehow ended up with a direct report.

"Jenny" (to spare both our blushes) had been hired to help with the corporate website. The consultancy, training, and product teams were all churning out new content that needed to be pushed onto the website. In the absence of any real clue about how to manage people, I fell back on the closest analogue I had: the military approach of barking orders. Wrong, wrong, wrong. In addition to coming across as a complete douchebag, I'd fallen into the trap of thinking that Jenny would instantly understand the website, its information architecture, and our publishing processes and would automatically work in exactly the same way I did. It hadn't occurred to me to give her sufficient time to settle in and understand what I needed her to do, and I was so unreasonably expecting such a high standard that her slow progress was bound to disappoint me.

This is decidedly not the way to manage someone. For starters, not only is barking orders a terrible approach in management, I'd forgotten that it's a pretty awful approach in the military as well. Even if you have the authority to order people to do what you want, you'll still achieve a better result if people *choose* to do what you suggest rather than being forced to do so. If people neither respect your authority nor agree with the request, there's always scope for them to drag their heels; they will feel no incentive to go the extra mile and will likely be overly literal, complying only with the letter of the request, not the intent. As many wise people have observed, true leaders serve the people they're responsible for and encourage them to fulfill their own potential. But don't mistake this humility for passivity—a leader is no pushover. Good management requires both understanding and resolve.

An approach I've found instructive in becoming a more personable manager has been the concept of situational leadership, introduced by business experts Paul Hersey and Ken Blanchard.* As a manager, you need to figure out which stage of learning each of your team members is in and adapt your approach to managing them accordingly. Bear

---

* Strictly speaking, the updated version of situational leadership described in the short book *Leadership and the One Minute Manager*. If you can get past the slightly patronizing tone, it's well worth a read. See the Further Reading section.

in mind that people might be at different stages for different tasks—someone may be absolutely fine running usability tests but may need coaching to become better at presenting.

Hersey and Blanchard's theory holds that when you start a new job or acquire a new skill, you go through different stages of learning with different associated levels of enthusiasm and stress.

1. **Unconscious incompetence:** Also known as the *Woohoo* stage. At this point you'll be saying to yourself, "Of course I can do this, I've done [*insert completely unrelated activity here*] before, so this can't be that hard, right?" Enthusiasm will be high and stress will often manifest as "butterflies" in the stomach.

2. **Conscious incompetence:** Also known as the *Ice-Cubes-Down-the-Back Wake-Up Call* or the *Trough of Realism*, in which enthusiasm plummets and stress rockets. At this stage, you're thinking that the job is a lot harder than you envisaged, you're not entirely sure why you decided to do it in the first place, and you're seriously considering handing back the scalpel/hazmat gear/riding crop and saying you're probably not qualified to do the task. This is where you show your true colors—if you can knuckle down and persevere, you *will* start to improve. Don't listen to the voices in your head telling you to give up.

3. **Conscious competence:** Also known as the *I'm Getting the Hang of This* stage. You're beginning to master the new skill, the bruises are no longer showing, and the various lawsuits have died down. You still have to think about how to do the task right, but it's getting easier every time, so your enthusiasm and stress levels are stabilizing.

4. **Unconscious competence:** Also known as the *Look Ma, No Hands!* stage—minimal stress, maximum enthusiasm. This is where you don't really have to think about the task anymore; you *feel* how to do it, like a Zen master. You can slow down time and dodge bullets, but it's still advisable to look where you're going to avoid it becoming the *Look Ma, No Teeth!* stage.

You can be fairly directive in your approach with newbies, because they're generally enthusiastic but have no clue what they're doing (unconscious incompetence). You can just tell them what you want and how you want it, and doing so doesn't take up too much of your time. But as they acquire a bit more competence, they hit the Trough of Realism and their commitment takes a big hit, so you need to devote more of your time to coaching them. This should involve a combination of telling them what you want and being more supportive to help them figure out how to do it for themselves. Then, as their confidence and competence improve, their enthusiasm will return, but it will still occasionally take a knock. So you should move into a mode of relying more on their judgment of what to do but still helping them when they get stuck. Be sure not to neglect these more competent team members. They can still require you to spend a reasonable chunk of your time providing support and reassurance. When they finally achieve mastery and their competence and commitment are both high, you can simply delegate work to them with the confidence that it will be done well, and the time you spend directly managing them will decrease.

Whatever happens, always have time for your team. If you have to work late because the needs of your team came first, so be it. The time, effort, and support you put into your team will more than pay for themselves.

ADAPTING YOUR APPROACH

The trick to adjusting your style lies in understanding the needs and the level of involvement in your product of each of the groups of people discussed in this chapter and adapting your approach to suit.

One way to think about this is to map out your product's various stakeholders on a grid similar to the stakeholder map shown. You're not trying to map out absolutely everyone here, just the main players. By meeting with each one, you'll start to assess how influential and interested they are in your product, and whether they're likely to be advocates, detractors, or on the fence. You'll then need to devote more

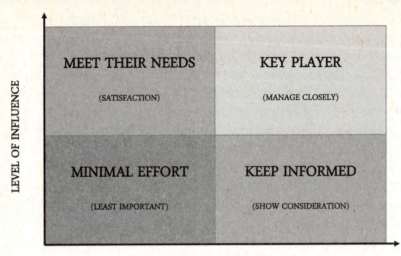

MEET THEIR NEEDS	**KEY PLAYER**
(SATISFACTION)	(MANAGE CLOSELY)
MINIMAL EFFORT	**KEEP INFORMED**
(LEAST IMPORTANT)	(SHOW CONSIDERATION)

LEVEL OF INFLUENCE

LEVEL OF INTEREST

Plot the people involved with your product on a stakeholder map. (Image concept courtesy of General Assembly)

time and effort toward managing the people with more interest and influence, whether they're supporters or critics. What may be surprising is that the more-senior managers in your organization may not all end up in the top-right quadrant. Your company's board of directors, for example, would clearly be highly influential, but may not need frequent updates, so would probably sit in the top-left quadrant. However, you'll need to manage more closely the board member to whom the product team ultimately reports, so that they can act as an advocate and supporter of your product on your behalf.

In contrast, the person running your technical support team is likely to be very interested in the progress of the product, but not necessarily directly influential on it, so would sit in the bottom-right block. However, if you're beginning to notice that everyone in your organization seems to be both highly interested and influential, you'll have your work cut out for you. That situation sounds suspiciously like design by committee, and you'll have an immensely difficult job reaching consensus to move the product forward. An even bigger challenge will be to gently negotiate some of the stakeholders into positions of lesser influence, freeing you to assert more control over your product and make decisions more easily. This is where good communication can make all the difference.

BETTER COMMUNICATION

Right at the beginning of this chapter, I mentioned that poor communication is responsible for much dysfunction within organizations. If people aren't exchanging information with each other well, how on earth can they expect to coordinate their efforts? With that in mind, it's always a source of bewilderment to me that we rely so heavily on email to communicate. Emails taunt us in our inbox, begging for attention. They follow us on our mobile devices. There is no respite. Most importantly, they're categorically *not* suited to all situations. So come a bit closer—I have some important advice for you: *you can also **talk** to people.*

As a general rule, product managers receive about four hundred to five hundred emails per week and respond to roughly half of them, which takes up about a third of their working lives. I bet a significant proportion of these emails could be avoided if the sender just picked up the phone or wandered across the office for a chat. Some people choose to hide behind emails as a way of avoiding unpleasant human interaction. If this is your view, I hate to be the one to point out that product managers are expected to speak to people occasionally; it comes with the territory. Emails aren't just addictive, they can lead to inefficiency. According to one study, each time we allow one to interrupt us, it takes more than a minute for us to recover our train of thought.[9] Dr. Tom Stafford notes in a 2008 article in *The Guardian*:

Both slot machines and email follow something called a "variable interval reinforcement schedule," which has been established as the way to train in the strongest habits. This means that rather than reward an action every time it is performed, you reward it sometimes, but not in a predictable way. So with email, usually when I check it there is nothing interesting, but every so often there's something wonderful—an invite out, or maybe some juicy gossip—and I get a reward.[10]

Similarly, Pulitzer Prize-winning journalist Charles Duhigg writes in his book, *The Power of Habit*:

When a computer chimes or a smartphone vibrates with a new message, the brain starts anticipating the momentary distraction that opening an email provides.... (On the other hand, if someone disables the buzzing—and, thus, removes the cue—people can work for hours without thinking to check their inboxes.)[11]

Here's why I'd be overjoyed if product managers all broke the email habit.

Emails Elongate and Confuse Discussions

Have you ever seen news reporters trying to interview someone with a satellite delay? That can be pretty confusing with just two correspondents. How badly do you think a similar lag between question and response would affect a discussion among a group of people?

When I'm Annoyed, I Read Emails with the Angry Voice in My Head

The absence of any visual cues (body language, facial expressions, etc.) means that a perfectly innocent email can suddenly take on a completely unintended tone, perhaps pointed, dismissive, sarcastic, rude, or the like. I believe this is called *projection*.

Emails Can Easily Be Taken out of Context

You don't actually know when someone is going to read your email, so sometimes the vital contextual link is lost in the intervening time between writing and reading. This doesn't contribute to ease of understanding.

Despite Years of Practice, I Still Cannot Type Faster Than I Can Speak

Emails waste my time. Phoning or speaking to someone in person is generally quicker, easier, and more effective. This is also why I shun instant messaging and will continue to be a refusenik.

Some People Expect an Immediate Response to Emails

Someone sends an email. They assume the recipient will see and open the email immediately, and so when they do not receive an immediate reply, they also assume they're being pointedly ignored. In reality, the recipient might just be doing something else.

Email Can Be Useful (Sometimes)

To be fair, email does have its uses. It's great for forwarding documents or factual information (dictating a document over the phone would be insane) and broadcasting a message to a large number of people. Sometimes you'll be conversing with someone whose first language is not English, and their written English may be better than their spoken English. And with some of your colleagues, both inside the company and out, it may be important to get communications in writing so you have a record. But generally, I recommend that if you can, go and speak to people. Get everyone in a room for fifteen minutes if you have to. You'll not only conclude the discussion more quickly, but you'll also get some lovely exercise by moving from your desk. And you'll get the benefit of *seeing* how people feel about the topic as well as listening to their reactions. Of course, you have to be selective, otherwise you'll end up in meetings all day. But failing to have face-to-face discussions leaves a great deal of potential communication unexpressed. Even a video call doesn't give you all the visual cues you get from physical presence.

SAYING NO

Most product managers hate saying no. It's not in our nature to disappoint people. We'd much rather give a nice, cooperative yes that makes everyone happy and leaves us feeling warm and fuzzy. The problem is that saying yes to everything creates manifest chaos. Whatever passed for a roadmap is effectively torn up and thrown out. You've made a commitment to deliver everyone's requests, which is a practical impossibility because some of them are almost surely conflicting or baseless.

Your role as a product manager is first and foremost to guide and shape the success and growth of your product. Being responsible for a product's strategy means that you have to make choices simply because attempting to do everything results in an unfocused mess. Just remember how companies succumb to "feature-rhea" because they think that more features equals more value. Product managers are duty bound to say no regularly, and what makes your response palatable here is the justification you offer. For parents, "Because I said so" may be an acceptable—or the only possible—retort, but it's never a good response for a product manager. Expect to point out the things that would have to be jettisoned to accommodate some shiny new flourish and how much additional budget and time you would need. Don't begrudge this approach; it's usually very effective. Even if people initially go off in a huff, the practicalities will eventually sink in. Also, when you have to say no, do so firmly, politely, and unambiguously. You may have to repeat yourself nonetheless, but the firmer you are the better. If you leave the door open even a crack, some people will try to bludgeon right through it.

MIND YOUR MANNERS

My folks brought me up to remember my manners. I concede that as a Brit I may take this a little too far. I sometimes find myself apologizing to people who have just barged into me on the streets of London. But manners and humility are vital for a product manager. Always remember that your success relies on the help of many others, and any one of them might do a great deal to derail the product, and thereby derail you.

Think of all the things people do for you: developers and designers have to guess what you mean in your user stories (short descriptions of the product features you want them to build) because often some context has been left in your head, and YOU ARE NEVER AT YOUR DESK. Marketing has to understand all the cool new things your product does and find the people who'll actually give a damn. The sales team has to penetrate all your product's technobabble and marketing fluff to find the trigger that will part clients from their cash. Finance has to figure out how your clever multitiered pricing model works to ensure that they're chasing the right clients for the right amounts and not breaking several impenetrable accounting rules. And tech support has to field calls from dozens of confused customers because a small but crucial feature has changed its behavior without any advance warning from you.

Product managers are by definition generalists across a broad spread of disciplines. It's essential that we rely on the depth of our team members' expertise; as much as we may know about sales, marketing, finance, user interface design, programming, or the latest technologies, we're not the experts. We've got to find a delicate balance between delegating to people who know much more than we do about the details and keeping on top of what they're doing and steering it. So be grateful for any help you receive from others. Thank them sincerely whenever you can, even if they're "just" doing their job. You will always need to call on them again, because you can't do your job without their help.

POINTS TO REMEMBER

You're Actually Managing People, Not Products

» Your product's success (and thus your own) is largely contingent on your ability to understand, communicate with, and influence others to help you, usually without direct authority.

» Cope with difficult individuals by being sympathetic to their frustrations and challenges. In the end, most people simply want to be recognized for their good work.

» Developers are miracle workers. They turn a product vision into reality and make it look easy.

» Good designers can take the complex and make it profoundly simple. Great designers will also stir your soul with the beauty of their design.

» Forge a productive relationship with the marketing team by sharing your market understanding with them and using their expertise in communicating with the market.

» Selling is *hard* and requires a certain mindset. Accept that salespeople are coin-operated and learn how to find the most mutually beneficial way of working with them.

» When managing others, appreciate that they will be at different levels of competence for different tasks and tailor your approach accordingly.

» One face-to-face conversation is worth a hundred emails.

» Remember that you will occasionally need to say no (politely and firmly).

Chapter 4

THE FINE LINE BETWEEN SUCCESS AND FAILURE

The practice of product management may have its roots in Neil Mc-Elroy and bath soap at P&G, but that hasn't prevented some of the highest-profile companies from creating doomed consumer products. You may remember some of these classic failures:

» New Coke was designed to compete with the sweeter-tasting Pepsi, but sparked such an outcry from loyal customers that it was promptly withdrawn and replaced by the original recipe.

» The Sony Betamax lost the feature war to VHS because it couldn't fit a movie on a single tape.

» The Ford Edsel couldn't live up to Ford's sustained prelaunch hype, had a name that sounded like "pretzel," and looked just plain weird.*

---

* "Weird" is an understatement. Some customers thought the front grille looked like a "vagina with teeth," according to Matt Haig's book *Brand Failures: The Truth About the 100 Biggest Branding Mistakes of All Time*, p. 21. See the Further Reading section.

Or what about the stomach-churning mental associations caused by ill-advised brand extensions such as Bengay Aspirin (that familiar, scented pain relief cream—in my mouth), Life Savers soda (sickly-sweet liquid candy—yuck), and Frito-Lay Lemonade (mmm, salty potato chip goodness, but in a sweet drink)? Each of these wonders was presumably thought at the time by its respective owner to be the "next big thing" for the brand, and each failed miserably. The litany of failed products is long and populated by failures that range from the outright laughable—celery-flavored Jell-O;[1] what kid (or self-respecting vegetarian) was going to eat that?—to the perversely tragic—in the 1970s and '80s, lawn darts were a fun and popular outdoor game, but they caused thousands of disfiguring injuries and three deaths before the Consumer Product Safety Commission eventually banned them.[2]

Consumer products have a notoriously high failure rate because their success requires mass-market appeal. They generally have to sell in very large quantities to offset the high costs of research and development, approval, and distribution for sale. This makes me glad that I work mainly with software products; in many respects they're much simpler to bring to market. In chapter 2, we looked at the Segway as a textbook example of a solution in search of a market problem. It failed to fulfill the original vision for the product for several common reasons: like the Ford Edsel, it couldn't live up to its hype; it was not needed by as large a segment of the market as its creators thought; and the creators neglected to check their assumptions, the main one being that it would be legal to ride. If we could just perform more effective, up-front research, perhaps the percentage of products that fail—the statistics for which vary wildly from one in three to nine in ten[3]—would be drastically reduced. But as the case of New Coke showcased so glaringly, the painful fact is that sometimes even extensive market research and product testing lead us astray. Coca-Cola had conducted two hundred thousand consumer taste tests to confirm that their new formula tasted better than classic Coke, but they had failed to appreciate the bigger picture of consumer devotion to the brand.

Schadenfreude over "What were they thinking?" failures is almost irresistible, and every product manager has his own list of favorite flops. Among my personal favorites is the attempt by French ball-point pen manufacturer BIC to introduce a terrifically patronizing range of pens branded "for her," leading to some of the most amusingly sarcastic reviews ever written on Amazon.[4] I also still chuckle about Coca-Cola's doomed attempt to introduce Dasani water to the UK. Right from the start, things went badly. Dasani's advertising inadvisably claimed the product was full of "spunk," the meaning of which in the UK is quite different from in the U.S. (referring to a bodily fluid generated during a certain "spunky" activity between couples, which shall not be named here).[5] The press had no end of fun with that. Then a spokesperson let slip in an interview that the water was actually purified, remineralized tap water. That sounded somehow perverse. The final nail in the coffin was the revelation that some of the supplies had been contaminated with the chemical compound bromate, which is suspected of being a carcinogen.[6] The PR damage was done. Dasani lasted just five weeks in the UK before being withdrawn.

Every product manager should know that failure is always a possibility, even with the most brilliant product concept and engineering. Just think again about that comparison of Segway and Glass and how hard it is before launch to determine whether a product like Glass will take off in the mass market. In this chapter, keeping in mind the lessons learned about assessing consumer demand and working effectively with the product team, we'll first take a look at an additional set of the most common ways in which product creation goes off the rails. Sometimes the key problems are not so much in the initial assessment of what the consumer needs, but in bringing the product to the right market at the right time, ensuring it will be profitable, and orchestrating a polished and coordinated launch. Although the product manager can never entirely control the whole product process, and no product manager can ensure success, no matter how experienced she is or how remarkable her knack for knowing the market, we do have a core set of practices with which we can do the best possible job of keeping the process of development and launch on course.

As mentioned before, there are many established frameworks for the product management process, each with its own best practices and formula, but in my experience, no two companies I've worked with have followed these methods in exactly the same way. That's why, as I've been doing throughout this book, I'll introduce the fundamentals rather than presenting a methodology to follow slavishly. In my experience, it's best for product managers to cherry-pick the right tools for a given company and job. The good news is that you will be able to employ the basic practices I'll be covering here irrespective of the framework you're using. And if the product doesn't manage to navigate to the right side of the fine line between success and failure, when you've applied these practices, you, your team, and higher-ups will know that the failure wasn't due to your simply allowing the wheels to fall off.

I started the chapter by referring to a set of notorious packaged goods failures. Well, the world of software products has its own special repository of unfortunate releases, and while some of them seem to have been clearly destined for consumer rejection right from launch—Apple Maps comes readily to mind—others have more complicated reasons for failure. Let's take a look at the most common reasons that products fall flat, with a special eye to some issues that are specific to software development and launch.

THE WHOLE PRODUCT MUST BE READY

When you think of the quality of a product, it's important that you think about not just the product your development team has built, but the *whole product* in the *Crossing the Chasm* sense, meaning the associated customer services, partners, and distribution channels as well. An otherwise perfect launch can be ruined by just one aspect of the whole product experience failing—this is why it's so difficult to get right. If you think about it this way, there are many ways in which a product can end up falling well below the required standard. It might be that the product only goes partway toward solving the desired problem, or the design is confusing to customers, or the product has been rushed out the door prematurely before the company, partners, and distributors are ready, or it still contains many defects. Time pressure can arise if the company sets itself a deadline (arbitrary or otherwise) and refuses to be flexible with it. Embarrassing premature launches can also happen if the company is too focused on responding to its competitors' movements, rather than having the confidence to hold on until the product is ready for release.

Apple Maps was a perfect example of this, and a rare launch misfire for the company. Despite initial coziness—Google's then-CEO Eric Schmidt had been on Apple's board at one point—relations between Apple and Google had become strained since Google released Android. Steve Jobs was livid, accusing Google of stealing Apple's ideas and saying he was going to "destroy Android."[7] The sticking point was that Google Maps had turn-by-turn navigation on Android, but not on iOS, and Google wasn't in the mood to give away one of Android's key advantages.[8] So with the release of iOS 6 in September 2012, Apple removed Google Maps from its App Store and replaced it with Apple's own software. However, as it soon became clear, Apple Maps had been rushed out the door and was far from ready. Landmarks like the Golden Gate Bridge were misplaced by miles, the Brooklyn Bridge looked like it had melted,[9] and trusting users were lured onto airport runways[10] and into the Australian desert.[11] The app had failed in its primary task—to help its users navigate accurately from point A to point B—so a few months later, Apple had to backtrack and allow Google Maps back into the App Store, whereupon Google's product became the most popular download overnight.

But wouldn't you consider Apple Maps to be a minimum viable product? Aren't MVPs just substandard products rushed out to market? Well, no, not if you're doing what you're meant to. If you remember, the key word is *viable*, by which we mean *commercially* viable. The product may solve only one small problem for a small niche market in a basic way, but it should still solve that problem completely; customers should be willing to part with hard cash for it to solve that problem.

Maps was a high-profile failure of product quality and uncharacteristic of Apple's usual attention to detail, but we see this exact problem happen time and time again with other companies. Either the core product itself is subpar, or a good product is let down by a painful whole-product experience. First impressions matter—don't rush a launch if the whole product is not ready.

MISSING YOUR WINDOW

While there's no benefit in rushing something out before it's ready, dawdling longer than you have to before entering a market can also be a sure path to failure, particularly if the market is a short-lived fad. Equally, jumping late into a well-established market is a little like diving into shark-infested waters—you've got to have a pretty serious advantage tucked away to survive for long against all those experienced competitors. While you're holding back, perhaps still plowing through a backlog of requirements that long ago ceased to be "must-have" for launch, your competitors will be launching more minimal but perfectly acceptable products that satisfy the market needs better than your nonexistent product. Or you may find that you've been in lockdown for so long building your product that when you finally emerge, blinking, into the sunlight, your customers' needs have evolved and your new product is already obsolete. It's one problem to enter the right market late, but it's an entirely different problem to pick the wrong market to enter in the first place. The market itself may be going away: you don't see many developers rushing to build native BlackBerry apps, for instance.

Thinking back to the Kano model, you'll remember that over time, distinctive delighters become linear satisfiers, then baseline features. This means a late-entry product must do more from the outset just to be permitted to compete in the market; differentiation from competing products will be more difficult, and commoditization means profit margins will be tighter. It's always a better idea to find the clear water of niche markets in which only your product can compete, even if only to begin with.

Keep a sense of urgency when planning to enter a new market. You don't necessarily have to be first, but you certainly don't want to be last. Be ruthless about initially delivering the minimum set of product features required to satisfy a basic market need completely, then learn from the feedback and iterate quickly to improve in the right areas.

STRETCHING OUTSIDE YOUR EXPERTISE

Many companies have tried to extend a brand farther than it should stretch—recall the attempts to sell consumers Life Savers soda and Frito-Lay Lemonade. In the computing products terrain, think of the Facebook phone. This isn't to say that brands don't have to extend into new areas, but they should do so by growing their expertise. Of course, this is much easier said than done, and sometimes companies just have to get into a new business and polish their expertise as they go. Microsoft is a good case in point. Its first-generation Surface tablet was largely a market failure, but the company made improvements for the next generation, and the Surface 2 was better received. It was important for Microsoft to build its consumer products business while the home PC market declined, and this was a calculated effort.

But you can also misstep badly if you naïvely attempt to enter a market too far removed from your company's area of expertise. Such initiatives often end up as distractions from your core product strategy and stretch resources and investment as you set about learning how the market works. There's a good reason most big players enter new markets by acquiring smaller, specialist firms—as Apple did with both iTunes and the iPod, and as Microsoft did with Nokia: it's the quickest way to gain niche market expertise, albeit a more costly option.

MAKING A FLAWED BUSINESS CASE

While a business case for your product will never be an exact predictor of the future, you should still be wary of models that depend on an unreasonably high sale price for mass adoption in the market or, conversely, indicate slim or nonexistent profits. You might recall the example earlier of Iron Mountain's "successful" backup service that lost money on every customer. Poor execution on the product delivery meant a crucial data compression feature was omitted, which in turn raised the operating costs sufficiently to negate the profit margin. A similar problem can arise if the sales team or retailers lack confidence in the product and are unable to articulate its value to different market segments or if competitive pressures result in a price war.

Another potential pitfall arises when even moderate success will be insufficient. If your business case relies on achieving exponential growth for the product to be considered a success, it's going to be much harder to achieve the high rate of customer acquisition needed. When thinking about the business model for your product, pay attention to the factors that may have the most impact on your profitability. Build three business cases: the best case (every variable factor is in your favor), the worst case (the reverse), and the most likely case. If the difference between best and worst cases is vast, there's still too much variability and risk in your model. Similarly, if only the very best case is profitable, pay attention to the red flag this presents.

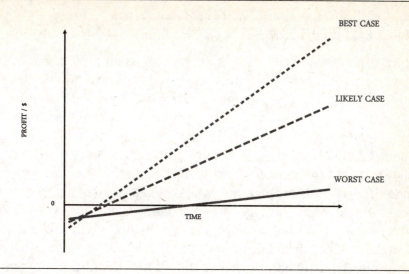

Model the best, worst, and most likely cases...

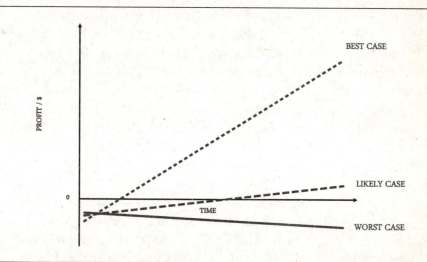

...and watch out for red flags like slim profitability. (Courtesy of Jock Busuttil)

WHAT WE HAVE HERE IS A FAILURE TO COMMUNICATE

One of the reasons product management is such a pivotal role in an organization is that without it, there would be no one who both appreciated the respective challenges and needs of each department and was responsible for actively sharing relevant information with all of them. People are rarely comfortable admitting they don't understand something, which is often why the building of good software is a mysterious process to many business executives. Products fail as a result of poor internal communication, when the left hand of an organization is unaware of what the right hand is doing—and has no interest in finding out. You must therefore speak frequently with all the different departments involved in the planning, creation, and delivery of your products. This can be one of the truly difficult parts of the job, because some people on the team may be reluctant to apprise you of problems they're running into and others will resent you for asking. As we discussed in chapter 3, if you're not communicating effectively across the company, the wheels will begin to fall off as each department starts diverging and doing its own thing rather than following the product plan. Not sure who you need to be talking to? Grab a company directory and cross your own name out. That's your list.

Meet with each team frequently enough that you can gather timely intelligence from them, keep them informed about relevant upcoming dates and product milestones, and ensure that any problems they have with the product—or indeed any problems they're causing—can be rectified before they blow up into something altogether less convenient. For some teams, this will mean a meeting every month; for others it may mean weekly or, in times of crisis, even daily meetings.

As we saw with the launch of Dasani's water in the UK, products can also fail as a result of ineffective or ill-judged external communication, whether through advertising, public relations, or social media. Ideally, the PR specialists you work with should be diligent enough to understand the product and its benefits, to tailor international launches to avoid embarrassing cultural gaffes, to coordinate messages across all communication channels, and to target the right messages to the right audiences. It's also a good sign if the launch campaign does not rely solely on the success of PR to sell the product, with budget available for other initiatives to promote the product not just at launch but later in the product's life as well.

To ensure a coordinated launch, make it your responsibility to prepare all the departments and partners involved in advance. Provide them with relevant information, in the form they need, at the right time to use it. It's also your job to whip everyone into a frenzy of excitement and expectation, which peaks with the launch of your product. (Just enough hype, though—you don't want the grand unveiling to be an embarrassing anti-climax, as befell Segway.)

LEARN FROM YOUR SUCCESSES

With the odd exception, like that of the Maps app, Apple has always been annoyingly good at product launches. When it launched the first iPad, the company sold one million units within the first twenty-eight days. More tellingly, it had also made sure the whole product was ready for launch: from the ecosystem of five thousand iPad apps already available, customers made twelve million downloads and bought 1.5 million ebooks from the iBookstore within the same period. And if you're thinking that the iPad launch success was due only to the product being a game changer, think again.

Looking at the iPhone's performance over the years, it's clear that Apple is good and getting better at launching product updates as well:

Product Model	Release Date	Launch Figures	Launch Countries	Average Sales per Day per Country
iPhone	June 29, 2007	1M in 74 days	1	14,000
iPhone 3G	July 11, 2008	1M in 3 days	22	15,000

(continued)

Product Model	Release Date	Launch Figures	Launch Countries	Average Sales per Day per Country
iPhone 3GS	June 19, 2009	1M in 3 days	8	42,000
iPhone 4	June 24, 2010	1.7M in 3 days	5	113,000
iPhone 4S	October 14, 2011	4M in 3 days	7	190,000
iPhone 5	September 29, 2012	5M in 3 days	9	185,000
iPhone 5S and 5C	September 20, 2013	9M in 3 days	11	273,000

Sources: Piper Jaffray; AppleInsider; Apple.

This improvement was not due purely to the acquisition of new customers. Apple was able to drive 77 percent of its day-one sales of the iPhone 4 from existing iPhone customers seeking an upgrade. I'm deeply envious—it's every product manager's dream to see his product fly off the shelves so quickly after launch. Then again, not every company is as good at preparing for a product launch as Apple. Apple is successful because it readies its people across the globe and coordinates all the moving parts for a single coherent and well-executed launch event.

Apple may make it look easy, but in practice a successful launch can be very difficult to orchestrate. I've found you can boost your chances of success by making a checklist of things that each internal department, your customers, and the partners will need to know and when. It won't be a short list. Naturally, these items will be specific to your own company, so work with your teams to create the list you need. Keep your launch checklist at hand and review progress at least weekly as you approach the launch date. Then, before the launch, assess how prepared your company, customers, partners, and target market are for the forthcoming launch by verifying whether they've digested the information you've sent out. You could also check with your distributors or sales team to find out how many preorders have been taken. After your launch, the data you've gathered will allow you to analyze the rate of sales, the proportion of existing customers upgrading, and the effectiveness of different channels to market, so you can repeat your success and improve your performance for next time.

CUSTOMERS AREN'T READY OR WILLING TO UPGRADE

A particularly challenging issue with software is that nothing ever stands still. We have to constantly contend with technological innovation in the ecosystem of products our product depends on or is designed to complement. We end up releasing an updated version of our product either to take advantage of a new opportunity or to respond to a significant change. But while we may become accustomed to change, our customers may not be so willing to move with the times. Even if you're shipping desktop or server software (as opposed to cloud-based web apps), eventually the operating system version on which your product runs will go away, and, in extreme cases, if you haven't stayed up to date the cost (and practicality) of porting ancient software to a new operating system may be prohibitive.

I once observed this very problem firsthand at a software supplier whose few remaining mainframe customers (mostly banks) had finally gotten around to upgrading their systems. They soon discovered that the original software didn't run on the new mainframe server. Although the software had lain untouched all these years, the customers had been paying for software maintenance throughout and so requested an updated version from the supplier. The complication was that the supplier had unwisely gambled on the customers' glacial pace of change and made its entire mainframe development team redundant several years earlier. The company no longer possessed the technical knowledge in-house to update the software in question. The options available were to lose the mainframe customers (expensive— particularly if they requested a refund for all those years of pointless software maintenance payments), to migrate the customers onto a working version of the software on a different operating system (impractical for the customers), or to find and recruit the necessary developers to update the software (time-consuming and costly). In the long run, the gamble of ignoring the customers stranded on the old version of the software (while the maintenance payments continued to roll in) had most certainly *not* paid off.

There are often perfectly sensible reasons why a customer may not want or be able to move up to the latest version every time you release. As Microsoft found out when they launched Windows Vista, aside from the user interface annoyances[12] and initial lack of support for printers and other peripherals,[13] the real killer of widespread adoption—particularly in the lucrative corporate market—was Vista's significantly increased hardware requirements over its predecessor, Windows XP. When deciding whether to upgrade everyone's desktops and laptops, corporate IT departments were having to factor in not just the operating system license costs, but also the wholesale costs of replacing aging machines with higher-spec hardware.[14] With IT budgets squeezed, the vast majority elected to skip Vista entirely when it was released in 2006 and wait until Windows 7 appeared. Several years later, over a quarter of users[15] were still clinging to XP right up until Microsoft finally killed it off in April 2014, possibly because the prospect of upgrading to Windows 8 was just as unappealing.

The timing of upgrades can be a major hurdle for some organizations. Rather than making changes as needed, the more risk-averse restrict major hardware and software alterations in their data centers to specific and relatively infrequent windows of opportunity. Some organizations have quarterly change windows; others have them annually or even less frequently, causing the changes needed to pile up in advance of each window. This often results in a highly complex upgrade process that requires weeks (if not months) of costly planning effort to execute correctly. So the controls these companies put in place to mitigate the risk of large changes can themselves cause the very problems they're meant to prevent.[16] If your customers have this kind of change management process in place, they're likely to take your product upgrades far less frequently than you release them, and so will need to make much bigger upgrade leaps each time. Correspondingly, any end-of-life schedule you create for your software may need to factor in the lead time needed before an appropriate window of opportunity opens up for your customers to perform their product upgrades.

You might think that cloud-based products pose less of a problem. After all, rather than each customer having their own separate copy of your product, everyone uses your central system, which you host and can update as you please. Well, not quite. Centrally hosted cloud services may make concerns such as the customer's operating system largely irrelevant, but you'll probably still need to have some concept of versioning as you continue to evolve your product. The convergence of web technologies to common standards may have made it easier to support multiple web browsers with a single product version, but at some point you'll want to make a significant change that will force you to decide whether to drop support for an outdated browser with idiosyncratic behaviors or continue to support it with a lower-tech version of your product alongside the more advanced mainstream version. Or perhaps you'll need to retire a feature entirely because it's preventing you from reworking some other aspect of your product. On the plus side, at least you'll be able to monitor directly who's using which feature with which browser and use that information to help you decide what to do.

A trickier problem arises when your customers are integrating directly with an application programming interface[17] (API) you provide. Think of your product's API as being the common language spoken by your product and your customers' systems, with the different functions the API provides being like the vocabulary. When you need to make a change to an existing function, it's a bit like suddenly deriding to substrate one wurzel for an apricot.* (Ahem.) Quite confusing, you'll agree. So it shouldn't be surprising that your customers' willingness to upgrade their integrations when you release a new version of your API will depend on how deeply they've integrated their systems with yours. You end up back at square one: you have to support multiple versions of your API in parallel until you can encourage your customers to upgrade their integrations to use the most recent version, and you still need to decide how long you're going to continue to maintain those older versions. Even cloud products need an end-of-life schedule.

One final gem of a reason why customers may refuse to upgrade to the latest version: discovering some salesperson has invented and sold them an "enterprise support contract" (committing the company to perpetual support for a particular product version), netted the sizable commission, then quit the company shortly thereafter before anyone realized what he'd done. As I learned the hard way, that makes for a fun day at the office.

YOUR CRUFT CATCHES UP WITH YOU

> **end-of-life** /ɛnd ɒv lʌɪf/ *v.* **to discontinue; drop; decommission;**
> **put out of misery; send to sleep with the fishes; take round the**
> **back and shoot; send the way of the Norwegian Blue.**

Product managers are full of contradictions: if we're not busting our asses to launch something, we're trying to kill our older products off. It may seem a little abrupt to leap straight from product launch to end of life, but the two go hand-in-hand. Like Apple with its iPhone customers, you ideally want your customers to move up to the newest version of the product, so for every major launch you need to be

---

* Translation: "It's a bit like suddenly deciding to substitute one word for another."

encouraging laggards to upgrade so that you can safely kill off the older product features or versions. But as we saw with Microsoft's launch of Windows Vista, this is easier said than done. It's important not to let the challenge make you complacent about identifying products that ought to be put out to pasture. Retiring a product is just like launching a product in reverse; much of your process and communication for orchestrating a successful product launch can be reused. And when you do need to put a product down, there are ways to do it humanely.

Many software companies have an annoying habit of accumulating "cruft." Cruft is that unpleasant mixture of dust, fluff, and other detritus that gathers in the corner of your sofa, underneath the cushions. It's also a fairly accurate description of all those legacy features or versions of your products that accumulate over time and are equally troublesome to get rid of. It is important to have a regular cleaning schedule to prevent the chronic buildup of cruft. In product terms, this means having a defined, published end-of-life process.

The key to a successful end-of-life program is transparency. If you're open with both internal stakeholders and customers about your plans to decommission products, there will be no unexpected surprises. And if everyone knows what's going to happen, they'll (hopefully) be more likely to accept progress as the status quo and fall into the routine of planning for it. It's therefore a good idea to determine how your end-of-life policy will work and share that with your customers. It doesn't need to be particularly complex; it just needs to clearly set out the mechanics of when and how you will retire products.

If you have several products that release new versions on a regular, periodic basis—perhaps you push out updates to your customers automatically—you may want to define a rolling end-of-life policy so you only ever have to support and maintain a small number of the most recent versions. This kind of rolling schedule could look something like the next figure.

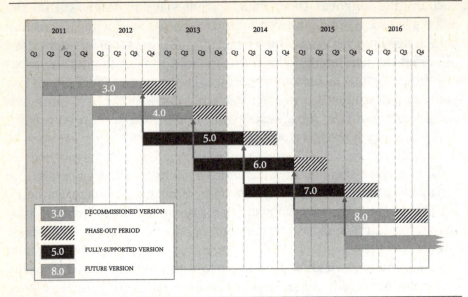

A rolling end-of-life schedule (Courtesy of Jock Busuttil)

In the diagram, when a major new version of a product is released, the version two releases ago moves into a six-month phase-out period and then is decommissioned. The advantage of this method is that your customers should always know that new releases automatically trigger older versions to move into the end-of-life process. Alternatively, if you release a relatively small and manageable number of products, or update them infrequently, you may want to retire them at your discretion. If you do adopt the latter model, its inherent unpredictability will make it much more important that you ensure your customers receive adequate warning to plan their upgrade.

THE SECOND ALBUM PROBLEM

Particularly for startups, another common problem is meeting high expectations set by a first product with the next product. Many successful startups suffer from the tricky "second album" problem. Like a breakthrough musician whose first album came out of nowhere and captured the mood of the moment perfectly, a startup may have had a first product that solved a market problem so neatly, and at just the right time, that in retrospect it is difficult to see how it possibly could have failed. Then it comes to the second product, but in the intervening time, a few things have changed about the company. For one, it's no longer a startup. It's an established business with a large, paying customer base to keep happy and a whole bunch of staff in formal departments, whereas before it was a ragtag handful of people all collaborating in the same room. The cofounders are busy dealing with their investors and advisors, perhaps debating whether to float the company publicly. They've lost touch with their roots, their market. They no longer inhabit the same world as their users, so they no longer have that direct source of insight that led them to hit the nail on the head with their first product. This is usually the point at which they conceive of their second product. As with the breakthrough musician who's left her roots behind for high-profile gigs, interviews, and parties, the follow-up simply lacks authenticity. Or, in product terms, it's based on the flawed assumption that the cofounders are still in tune with the sentiment of their market. And since the expectations of the market were raised by the first product, the follow-up product not only has to resonate with the audience, but also has to be *even better* to meet those new expectations. It's no wonder that the second product (or album) is often a let-down.

That's quite a daunting set of problems to watch out for, and of course it's not exhaustive. There are many more ways for a product to fail than there are products. So the question is, how does a product manager keep on top of all of these things, make sure the development and launch are proceeding apace, and avoid pitfalls?

BEING AGILE

Traditional product development employed a "closed-box" approach that offered little insight into progress and typically could only sacrifice quality, as both time (i.e., money) and the scope of requirements were set in stone. The process was understandably stressful for the hard-pressed development team, who often had the unappealing choice to either fail against the criteria set by senior management or deliver substandard products. In contrast, Agile development offers stakeholders a more granular and transparent view of progress, and offers the development team the flexibility to hit deadlines while maintaining quality, as long as the scope is left to the best judgment of the product owner. The stress of meeting deadlines is therefore shouldered by the product owner, but she is empowered to manage the team's work to allow a timely delivery. "Good enough to launch" doesn't have to mean "build everything, including the kitchen sink."

One of the most common styles of Agile product development is Scrum, which is explained succinctly by its creators, Ken Schwaber and Jeff Sutherland, in *The Scrum Guide*.[18] Product manager and Agile coach Roman Pichler describes the main differences between the traditional ("Old School") and Agile ("New School") methods of product management on his blog:[19]

Old School	New School
Several roles, such as product marketer, product manager, and project manager, share the responsibility for bringing the product to life.	One person—the product owner—is in charge of the product and leads the project.
Product managers are detached from the development teams, separated by process, department, and facility boundaries.	The product owner is a member of the Scrum team and works closely with the Scrum master and team on an ongoing basis.

Old School	New School
Extensive market research, product planning, and business analysis are carried out up front.	Minimum up-front work is expended to create a vision that describes what the product will roughly look like and do.
Up-front product discovery and definition: requirements are detailed and frozen early on.	Product discovery is an ongoing process; requirements emerge. There is no definition phase and the product backlog evolves based on customer and user feedback.
Customer feedback is received late, in market testing and after product launch.	Early and frequent releases together with sprint review meetings generate valuable customer and user feedback that helps create a product customers love.

In Scrum, a product is developed over several *sprints*. A sprint is a time-boxed period of development, usually a month or less but always the same length, during which a potentially releasable product increment is created. The *product owner* is a specific role within Scrum, usually played by the product manager, that is solely responsible for determining which items go on the *sprint backlog*, a list of discrete, specific, and bite-sized pieces of work for the product. For each item on the backlog, the product owner and development team together describe in *user stories* how and why the intended user persona needs to interact with the product. Together they also score the relative complexity of each user story in *story points*. Backlog items are intended to be small items of work because those are easier to estimate and complete than one massive piece of work (an *epic*—so-called because it's a very large user story). The product owner ensures the team tackles the highest-priority items first by placing them at the top of the backlog. Scrum establishes a routine for the development team that makes sprints predictable and allows the developers to focus on what they do best—building product. As you've hopefully noticed by now, a product manager has a variety of responsibilities, of which being the product owner is but one, so good time management is needed to avoid having the product owner role take up all your attention.

Once your development team has settled into its routine (or *cadence*), you can measure its velocity each sprint as a means of predicting when a product will be ready. Velocity is simply a measure of how many backlog items the team can implement in a given time, as measured by totaling the story points of the items completed. You may find, as I have, that the more frequent release of incremental product updates can mean that nobody (neither your company nor your customers) notices their arrival. It's therefore a good idea to make a bigger splash (a formal launch) every now and again to draw your market's attention to the improvements you've made, even if they've already been released into the wild and particularly if there's a coherent story or theme behind a group of improvements. If you know your team can generally do about twenty story points' worth of work in a two-week sprint, and you know there are roughly sixty points' worth of work outstanding that must be done before you can make your big-splash product announcement, then you also know that your launch is roughly six weeks away, all things being equal. This approach assumes you're not changing the development team members around each time and that they're reasonably good at estimating story points (which they should be after a few sprints).

Bear in mind a couple of important points. It's natural for velocity to vary a little from sprint to sprint, so think of it more as a rule of thumb than a to-the-minute-accurate predictor of product delivery time.[20] Also, Agile processes tend to focus on providing detail on short-term activities (current and next sprints at most), so you won't have detailed estimates for far-off items. This approach is sometimes known as *horizon planning*. It saves you time in the long run because your plan is continually evolving as you learn more about your product and market from incremental releases, so there's no point in planning far ahead in more detail than is necessary.

PRIOR PREPARATION AND PRODUCT PLANNING PREVENT POOR PERFORMANCE

Your overall product strategy is the combination of many different activities with short-term, medium-term, and long-term focuses, such as determining future product requirements based on your ongoing market research or reviewing pricing strategy in light of changes to the market and competitor activity. You can zoom in on each of these activities and find more detail—for feature requirements you might be thinking about the user personas they apply to, breaking epics into smaller user stories, and guerrilla testing your assumptions with a few customers and a quick product mockup before you move into developing them.

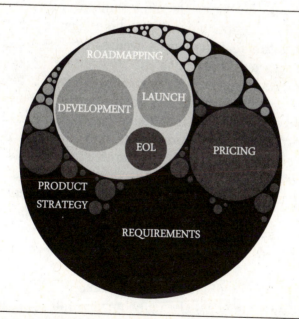

There are many different activities competing for a product manager's attention. (Courtesy of Jock Busuttil)

Seeking Out Lightbulb Moments

Another day, another fire to put out—it's all too easy to get lost in the day-to-day tasks. But your market research is never done. One of the best ways to be blindsided by product problems is to hide at your desk and fiddle with spreadsheets and documents all day. The foundation of good product management is to get out there and talk to people. With the crush of work from managing internal stakeholders and the ongoing development process, one of the biggest challenges for product managers can be finding the time to escape to speak to the market regularly. You need to keep on with your wide-angled research by listening to the challenges faced by potential and existing customers, partners, suppliers, and regulators, in some cases; you should always be on the lookout for clues that may lead to good, new product ideas. But you should also be taking the opportunity to focus on validating the more specific assumptions you're making about products already under way—does this feature or that process work as intuitively and smoothly as users would expect?

There's no hard and fast rule for how often you need to get out there, but if you can manage to have at least a few decent conversations each week, that will increase your likelihood of experiencing "lightbulb" moments. These are the moments that highlight that you've been thinking about the market or your product in a particularly constrained way without even realizing it—like in cartoons, the metaphorical lightbulb illuminates above your head. Lightbulb moments are immensely positive experiences because they expand your world view and open up a wealth of creative options that you'd previously not even considered. The more lightbulb moments you experience, the better.

Then, to close the feedback loop, periodically test your thinking. There's a saying that you only truly understand something when you're able to explain it to someone else. So go back to your market and internal stakeholders with what you've learned to check whether you're on the right track. You could write articles for your company's blog and seek feedback; you could run seminars in person or online; you could engage in conversation with your market on social media or on relevant discussion groups. There's really no excuse these days for failing to present and discuss your ideas on a regular basis. Your objective is to pinpoint the ideas that will form the bases of potential new products or features. You can simply add new features low down on your product backlog until further investigation raises their priority. For new products, I recommend using a tool like the Business Model Canvas,[21] shown in the next figure, to structure your thoughts quickly without the need for a lengthy business case document.

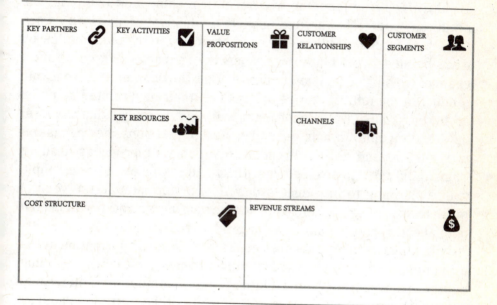

The Business Model Canvas (Courtesy of Business Model Foundry AG)

In order to achieve the right flow of new ideas, I'd recommend you aim to research and present at least one new idea each month. Making time for such regular presentations may seem impractical, but it's important to keep in mind that if you hide indoors while a current suite of products is in development, you won't be learning anything new and you'll almost certainly miss a change in the market or competitors for the products you're working furiously to launch.

Communicating Your Product Plan with a Roadmap

If the features are the "what" of the product, the roadmap is the "when." Your product roadmap serves a number of purposes. At its most basic, a roadmap is a communication tool for coordinating different groups of people. Just as a GPS unit guides you while driving to avoid traffic, your roadmap will be an invaluable aid to guiding your product's progression around unexpected holdups. This is why it's so important for there to be a degree of flexibility in the plan to allow for items being delivered later (or sooner) than expected—circumstances change. If you give people an idea of what they can expect from your product in the future, they're able to plan their own related activities around it. Your development team will need to know what's coming up in the medium to long term. The design decisions they're making now may depend on the direction in which your product's heading. They might need to hire people with specific skill sets if, for example, you're planning to introduce a new iPhone app later in the year. In much the same way, other teams within your organization will need to plan ahead to prepare for a major product release.

With all its various audiences and their differing information needs, a roadmap has to be a reasonably high-level view of how the product will evolve over time. You could use your roadmap to highlight both when new features will arrive and when it will be possible to address a new market segment. You can think of your roadmap as the story arc of your product, with major themed product releases being like chapters of a book, development sprints like sections, and individual product requirements like paragraphs, all consistent with your overall vision. But unlike with a book, you only need to worry about filling in the detail for a chapter or two at a time. Things change, not least because you're continually learning from the market, so there's little point in planning a release in detail for two years from now. Once you have your roadmap as a high-level timing guide allowing each team within your company to plan ahead, you can dive into the detail needed to satisfy different teams' processes on the more immediate items. You might have a roadmap item to introduce a native iPhone app, so as that item approaches you will need to supply much more detail than the roadmap provides: user stories and mockups to the designers and developers, benefits and features to the marketing team, pricing and licensing details to the sales team or partners, and so on.

Some roadmaps have specific dates on them and read a little like Gantt charts. If you're bound by very specific deadlines—perhaps your product needs some special certification, assessed only once a year, before it can be sold—this can be a perfectly reasonable approach. In other situations, such as in a startup, your primary constraint is money, rather than time, so you strive to do as much as you can before the money runs out. Ideally, the guiding factor for releasing a product should be *when it's ready*. But if you're time bound, when progress is behind schedule and it's coming down to the crunch, remember that you'll have to start sacrificing features from scope (or quality—not recommended) to keep to the deadline. If you're working in an Agile way, you should have a reasonably good idea of how quickly the current development sprint is progressing, and your sprint backlog will already have the most important requirements at the top of the list to be done first. Mind the Product cofounder Janna Bastow provides a similar roadmap as shown in the next figure in the form of an Excel template.[22]

Not everyone agrees with the time-based approach to roadmapping, which may seem bizarre; after all, isn't roadmapping about planning how long products will take to develop and when to launch? Veteran product manager and former space engineer Simon Cast points out in his blog post "Roadmapping Without Dates" that by setting such firm dates, you can shoot yourself in the foot.[23] Estimated dates have by

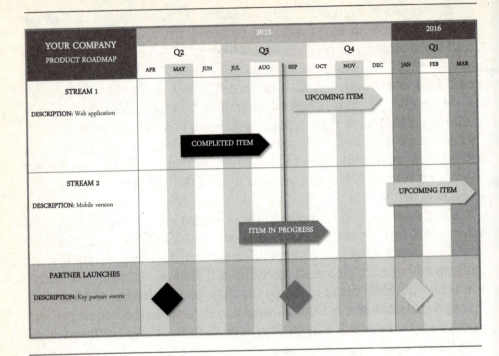

A *time-based style of roadmap (Courtesy of Janna Bastow, who provided a similar roadmap as a simple Excel template: "Tame Your Roadmap," Mind the Product, September 27, 2011, http://www.mindtheproduct.com/2011/09/tame-your-roadmap/)*

nature a degree of variability, and product managers recognize that fact, so the point at which a *specific* date is added to a roadmap is also the point at which everyone *except* the product manager believes the item in question will be delivered. It doesn't matter how you caveat the date ("It's a plan, not a promise"), it becomes gospel. Suddenly, you are judged by whether you meet the entirely fictitious dates, and that judgment doesn't take into account changing priorities or potential holdups.

Cast describes how ProdPad, the company he cofounded with Janna Bastow, started with the date-based approach but later moved to a no-dates roadmap divided into less specific timings: current, near-term, and future.[24] This approach can often require a change of corporate mindset in much the same way that Agile product development does.

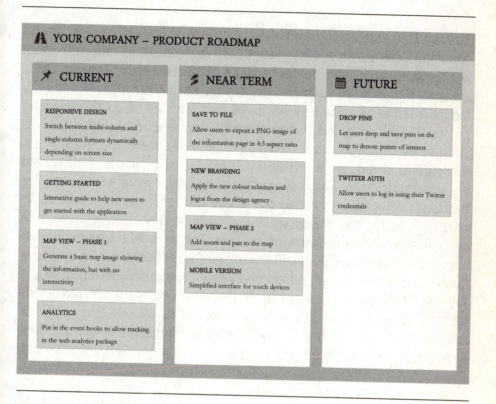

Product management tools such as ProdPad will generate these kinds of no-dates roadmaps for you. (Courtesy of ProdPad)

Of course, you do need to have a long-term destination defined for your product, along with a rough idea of when you expect to arrive there, but if you can work with more flexibility this way, you are better able to change course and make adjustments as may be needed due to market changes or development bottlenecks. New information will often become available and priorities will change, so you're going to have to review your roadmap at least every month to adjust course if necessary.

When Correcting Course, Tell People

If you do need to change the route midway, make sure there's a good set of reasons for doing so and write them down. Flexibility and good decision-making are far more important than clairvoyance (or blind luck). Test the assumptions you're basing your decisions on as quickly as possible to reduce risk without sacrificing your agility in the face of change. Then always be sure to come up with a new plan, rather than just raising a red flag that there's a problem. Update your stakeholders, customers, and partners on what's coming up, why it's important for them, and when it's coming. It doesn't necessarily matter if things move around on the roadmap as long as everyone is kept up to date, and those who need to know why things have changed understand the reasoning. There's a beautiful example of a customer-facing roadmap over at FreeAgent that allows people to vote on the features they're interested in; note that it has no dates, either—items are listed simply as "At Depot," "En Route," or "Delivered."[25]

Bear in mind also that the more complex your ecosystem of dependent partners and customers is, the more warning you need to give about changes. If, for example, hundreds of customers and partners have integrated your product directly into their own systems, arbitrarily changing it without warning in a way that would break their integrations would not make you flavor of the month. It's vital that you be sure you're giving sufficient warning to the people who will be affected most by roadmap changes and that you confirm they've understood the implications. It's also useful to measure their reactions to forthcoming items as a sense check—are they in favor, dead set against, or simply not interested either way? What you learn will inform how you prioritize future items on your roadmap, but remember that you can't please all of the people all of the time—compromises and sacrifices are sometimes necessary.

AVOID EPIC FAILURES BY PRACTICING SMALLER ONES

There's a reason why trainee pilots start out by repeating hundreds of takeoffs and landings: those are two of the riskiest parts of the entire flight. They both demand a high cognitive workload that is only increased by poor weather conditions, and if something goes wrong with the aircraft at these crucial times, there are precious few seconds for the pilot to react to and deal with the situation safely. So pilots practice and practice and practice. Then they practice some more. They practice engine failures immediately after takeoff, when the aircraft doesn't even have enough height or speed to turn back to land on the runway, and they practice landings without engines or working flaps or radios. They do this not because the likelihood of any or all of these things happening is high, but because the consequences can be so dire. Rather than avoiding the riskiest elements of a flight, pilots take those elements of risk and meet them head-on.

Working as a product manager in technology is—thankfully—almost never a matter of life and death. This, however, can make us complacent. One way to avoid this danger—which can lead to unexpected surprises when a product goes badly off the rails—is to regularly simulate failures. Eric Ries's Lean Startup methodology speaks of "failing fast," the idea that if you're uncertain whether your idea's going to work, it's better to find out quickly and cheaply. Such controlled failure gives us the opportunity to learn how to recover quickly from a failure and, ideally, how to avoid making the mistake in the first place. You only need to roll out a poorly tested release on a Friday evening once to learn that customers don't appreciate a weekend's disrupted service. But if you're regularly practicing your process for rolling back a flawed release, then it's far less of a problem to manage when it ends up happening for real.

Some product people even provoke failure in their live systems as a way to present more opportunities to learn. Google has teams of people devoted to exploring innovative ways to bring down their own services on the basis that if someone's going to try it, their preference is that it's a Google employee rather than a cybercriminal. Netflix, the online TV and film streaming service, has gone one step further and created a piece of software called the Chaos Monkey that deliberately knocks out components to test their automated disaster recovery. Cory Bennett, a senior software engineer at Netflix, and Ariel Tseitlin, former director of cloud solutions at Netflix, introduce the Chaos Monkey:

In most cases, we have designed our applications to continue working when an instance goes offline, but in those special cases that they don't, we want to make sure there are people around to resolve and learn from any problems. With this in mind, Chaos Monkey only runs within a limited set of hours with the intent that engineers will be alert and able to respond.

Failures happen and they inevitably happen when least desired or expected. If your application can't tolerate an instance failure would you rather find out by being paged at 3am [*sic*] or when you're in the office and have had your morning coffee? Even if you are confident that your architecture can tolerate an instance failure, are you sure it will still be able to next week? How about next month?[26]

HOW TO RESPOND TO A CRISIS

No matter how much we practice failing, there's no way around the fact that some snafus are inevitable. When the worst does happen, we have to think fast to figure out how to resolve the problem. We can end up panicking ineffectually rather than falling back on our training and reacting calmly. But we don't have to live in fear of failure—or of taking risks. In *The Power of Habit* Charles Duhigg describes NASA's response to failing:

> Some departments at NASA, for instance, were overhauling themselves by deliberately instituting organizational routines that encouraged engineers to take more risks. When unmanned rockets exploded on takeoff, department heads would applaud, so that everyone would know their division had tried and failed, but at least they had tried. Eventually, mission control filled with applause every time something expensive blew up.[27]

A crisis—literally a "turning point"—can also be an opportunity in disguise. (However, I would hasten to add that the oft-cited meme that claims the Chinese word for "crisis" is made up of the words "danger" and "opportunity" is complete bunk.[28]) It presents you with the chance to demonstrate your true colors by the way you perform under pressure. Furthermore, sometimes only a crisis can disrupt the equilibrium of a company stuck in a habitual rut, permitting positive change to occur. Later in *The Power of Habit*, Duhigg describes how repeated surgical errors at Rhode Island Hospital became a catalyst to overhaul safety procedures in 2009, improving staff relations and reducing the "wrong-site" errors rate to zero in the process. (Wrong-site errors are situations in which the surgeon operates on the wrong side or site of the body.) He also explains how the tragic 1987 fire at King's Cross station allowed London Underground to break down the silos of bureaucracy in order to make passenger safety its primary concern.

So how should you respond to a crisis? First and foremost, keep your head while all about you are losing theirs. You can expect a great deal of managerial pressure on you to act. Keep your nerve. Knee-jerk reactions and snap decisions will lack sufficient information and be likely to exacerbate the problem. Instead, take control of the situation by making yourself its owner; ultimately, most people want someone to take the heat from them, so they will be more than happy to relinquish responsibility to you. Overcommunicate throughout: If you're investigating something, explain what and where it is. If you're testing a potential fix, detail who's running the test and when you'll know the outcome. Provide your bosses with such frequent updates—even if only to report no change—that they beg you to stop. Remember that in the absence of information, people make up something to fill the void, and it's usually wrong. Avoid the blame game, as it's never constructive, and instead focus on figuring out the immediate cause of the problem and rectifying it. In doing so, you may uncover a deeper malaise that will need longer-term attention, but put this to one side for now.

Once you have a potential fix for the problem, test it first; there's nothing worse than raising people's hopes for a resolution only to dash them soon after. Roll out the fix to a small segment of those affected as a further test; you don't want to start a different fire inadvertently. When you're satisfied that you've solved the problem without significant side effects, roll out the fix to everyone else. Then pull together the people from the disciplines involved whom you'll need to resolve the underlying problem permanently. Again, avoid the blame game. Was it a one-off or a systematic problem? What do you need to start or stop doing to prevent it from happening again? If you can't prevent it, how can you receive earlier warning when the problem is still in its incipient stages? Ensure that the necessary improvements are implemented as quickly as possible; wait too long and the collective pain will subside, meaning people will lose the impetus to change. It's a little like how parents teach young children not to do daft things and hurt themselves; the lesson can only be learned while the scuffed knees still ache.

Sometimes people misunderstand the Lean concept of failing fast as giving them carte blanche to try out lots of different things really quickly (good), but in a haphazard, scattergun manner (bad) and without learning from each failure (worse). As Marc Andreessen said in an interview with the *Wall Street Journal*,

This whole thing where failure is somehow good in Silicon Valley, or failure is OK, or failure is wonderful, or failure is part of the process, is just a bunch of nonsense, and is actually a destructive sort of meme because it gives people an easy excuse to give up. If you look at a lot of the great successes in corporate history and in technology, they required real determination and real staying power.[29]

I can understand the sentiment Ries is trying to convey by using the word *failure*: taking a risk is not, in itself, a bad thing; fear of failure should not stop you from having a go anyway. However, some people can't get past the word because they've been conditioned to avoid failure at all costs, when really all it represents is the concept of invalidating a hypothesis or demonstrating with evidence that a held assumption was false. So maybe instead of *failing fast*, it's better for us to think of *learning fast*. You're only going to fail for sure if you learn nothing as you go along.

As I've mentioned before, product managers' ability to absorb knowledge is one of their most important traits, and this ability includes learning from mistakes. I was once interviewing candidates for a senior product manager role and was listening to one candidate tell his backstory of how he'd driven his previous company into the ground by forsaking all his other customers to risk everything on a single massive deal that never came through. When I asked him what he'd do differently next time, he replied, "Nothing." He didn't make it to the second round. Even in failure, there should always be something you can learn that will allow you to improve for next time. While describing Google X's rapid prototyping process for Glass, Tom Chi explained how he told his team to think not in terms of failing, but in terms of learning:

I don't believe in failing fast. Failing is just an approximation of learning. You can fail a lot without learning at all. And you can learn a lot without failing at all....Don't tell me this experiment failed or that experiment failed, tell me what was the twelve percent that worked.[30]

There may be a fine line between success and failure, but you can choose to step over the line on your own terms. And when things do go wrong—and they will from time to time—your training and experience will enable you to be the one calm head and voice of reason in the room. That's what being a product manager allows you to do.

POINTS TO REMEMBER

The Fine Line Between Success and Failure

» Failure is always a possibility: an otherwise perfect launch can be ruined by just one aspect of the whole product experience. Launch when you're ready.

» Don't step too far outside your company's core expertise. Obtain specialist skills you're lacking.

» Be realistic about the best, worst, and most likely outcomes of your business case, and pay attention to red flags such as slim profit margins.

» Effective communication, both internally and externally, is vital for launch coordination and ensuring that the right message reaches the right people.

» Prior preparation and planning prevent poor product performance.

» Practice failures to learn how to recover from them or avoid them in the first place.

» Always be learning, whether from your successes or failures.

Chapter 5
TENDER LOVING CARE OF TIME

———

> I love deadlines. I like the whooshing
> sound they make as they fly by.
> —*Douglas Adams*

Management guru Peter Drucker wrote in his book *The Effective Executive*, "Everything requires time. It is the only truly universal condition. All work takes place in time and uses up time. Yet most people take for granted this unique, irreplaceable, and necessary resource. Nothing else, perhaps, distinguishes effective executives as much as their tender loving care of time."[1] Drucker may have had effective executives in mind when he wrote that, but the same applies for product managers. We've explored a product manager's place at the intersection of the three rings of stakeholders and how it requires juggling the competing needs of the users, the business, and the technologists. It also requires juggling time.

Being at the center of things means you'll always be the best person for all those around the company to ask about your product, and people will almost constantly want five minutes of your time for "a quick question." In addition, the job requires keeping your eye on the longer-term strategy and direction for products, but the time you allot for this can be swallowed up by the press of immediate concerns.

This is why another ability that all good product managers need is one they share (somewhat improbably) with military pilots. To allow pilots to keep their attention on the outside world, rather than their aircraft's displays and controls, many planes have a special transparent, helmet-mounted display that superimposes targeting information and flight data over part of the pilot's field of vision but still leaves the wearer free to focus on what's going on outside the cockpit. In a similar way, product managers need to be able to switch their attention at will and swiftly between the concerns of the here-and-now and what's looming on the horizon. In an ideal world, you'd hope to be devoting about 80 percent of your attention to long-term planning and the remainder to the short term. (If you think about it, there is a great deal more *future* than *present*.) However, since the real world rarely follows the script, it's easy to find yourself spending most of your time putting out the fires that crop up on a day-to-day basis, leaving you little time to plan for the future. Start to add in the varying demands of multiple products, all at different stages of their life cycles, and it should be clear that mastering time management is vital for product managers.

At this point, you may be concerned because, let's be honest, product management sounds like it can be a logistical nightmare. The job can seem outright insane at times, and the juggling act it requires has prompted some people to suggest that it should in fact be divided into two jobs, product owner and product manager, with the product owner responsible solely for keeping on top of the development team and the product manager responsible for interacting with the other departments and customers. I agree, however, with product management guru Marty Cagan, author of the book *Inspired: How to Create Products Customers Love.* Cagan argued in a post on the Silicon Valley Product Group blog that such a division runs the risk of having no clear owner of the product creation process, and of breeding contempt between the two roles. But the most important problem, Cagan points out, is that splitting the role means that there is no one person that combines both customer empathy with technical know-how when making product decisions. As he writes,

> It is precisely this combination of deep customer understanding with the ability to apply technology to solve customer problems that enables a strong product person.[2]

I also believe that it's perfectly possible, and preferable, for the same person to play both roles. You might be daunted by the level of personal organization you're going to need to perform the role without dropping any balls. But let me reassure you: with practice, even the most terminally disorganized person can learn to organize herself. I can make this bold claim because I'm a prime example. One of the many professional challenges I've faced has been to overcome my natural tendency toward being disorganized. I have a horrible memory for dates and am the sort of person who's a little vague about what day of the week it is. While working late one night, I received a phone call from my girlfriend at the time inquiring whether I would be joining my birthday celebration with friends, which I'd totally forgotten about. I eventually compensated for my inability to remember dates by finding someone who could and immediately marrying her. Cunningly, I managed to propose on the anniversary of us first going out with each other, and we got married exactly one year later. As a consequence, I now have only one important date to remember (though, of course, the implications of forgetting that date are much more dire).

The problem of my poor time management at work was trickier to solve, since Lovely Wife gracefully declined to accompany me to work each day to remind me what I was supposed to be doing. Nor am I privileged/well paid/important enough to have an executive assistant. Yet in spite of my haphazard nature, over the years I've been able to adopt time management techniques and form habits that have helped me operate more like (or at least do a passable impression of) a normal, organized human being.

Learning to protect your time and apportion it well is crucial. It's easy to become overwhelmed, and every product manager will be at some point. So you must know how to dig yourself out. I sincerely hope you have a slightly less intense working experience than I did at Experian, which was the job that put me to the worst test. My team was responsible for more than twenty software products and forty or so packages of reference information shipped in different combinations with the software. The software products were of varying ages, each used by hundreds of customers, and some were stable, others needed some love and attention, and a couple were so defect-ridden that they would virtually burst into flames without warning. (That's figuratively speaking, but the customer responses really could be described as inflamed. When questioned about the issue, a developer helpfully responded, "Yeah, customers shouldn't click that button. It crashes the product immediately.") On the data side, we gathered reference sets from thirty-odd suppliers, all of whom were periodically updating their respective data sets, meaning we had to incorporate their changes and rebuild each data set in our proprietary format, otherwise we'd be shipping outdated data. When I joined, all of this was managed by a product team of twelve. By the time I left four years later, we were looking after the same set of products, plus a few new ones, with a team of only four. By necessity, we'd had to become extremely proficient at triage and time management. I've learned a number of techniques in my trials by fire for both.

DOING THE RIGHT THINGS AT THE RIGHT TIMES

Have you ever found yourself dreading writing that report or business case? Even if you have a template that gives you the headings of the sections you're expected to complete, these can be a real pain to work through. Whether it's a character trait of product managers in particular or a more general behavior, I've found that these kinds of information-heavy documents become much easier to write if the headings are expressed as open questions rather than statements. So for example, if one of the sections in your document reads, "Q4 Financial Performance," change it to read instead, "How has your product performed financially in Q4?" You should find that the answer flows much more easily.

Knowing When to Do Things

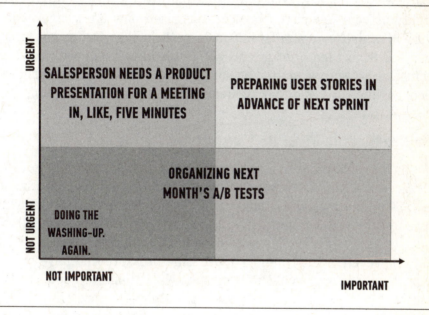

A quick triage tool for identifying the most urgent and important tasks to complete (Courtesy of Jock Busuttil)

Not all tasks are born equal. Some are more urgent than others, and some are definitely more important than others. In the heat of things, it can be easy to forget whether you're devoting time to the most urgent *and* important tasks, so it can be helpful to quickly sketch out what's on your plate right now using a grid similar to the one shown here. (Hint: do the top-right tasks first.)

Sometimes it is beneficial to pause before embarking on a task. In his book *Wait: The Art and Science of Delay*, professor of law and finance Frank Partnoy describes how sporting professionals learn to delay playing their shot until the last possible moment, as even these few short milliseconds of extra information convey an advantage over players who make their move sooner.[3] When you're deciding whether to act, taking an extra moment, minute, or couple of days—if you have that luxury—to absorb more information will ultimately improve the quality of your decision. You'd be surprised how often emergencies arise in which everyone involved is certain that the product manager needs to take charge and act immediately, yet which resolve themselves within a matter of hours when a little more information becomes known. Avoid making decisions as a knee-jerk reaction.

Use Deadlines to Motivate Yourself

In a biting article in the *Economist* in 1955, British naval historian C. Northcote Parkinson introduced what's become known as Parkinson's Law. The law states (with tongue firmly in cheek) that "work expands so as to fill the time available for its completion."[4] This means that if you give yourself a few hours to do something, that's how long it will take. However, if you're under more time pressure and have only an hour to get it done, you'll still most likely be able to complete it in time. If you've ever found yourself putting off a task until the last possible moment (who hasn't?), finishing it, and then finding yourself wondering why you didn't get it done so efficiently weeks ago, you'll know the phenomenon. If, like me, you need the motivation of looming deadlines, get proactive about them and use them to your advantage. You may find that just putting a reminder in your calendar isn't sufficient (I tend to ignore those), so go one step farther and promise someone that you'll have it ready for them. Now you've committed yourself, and you'd hate to let someone down, wouldn't you?

DEALING WITH COMPLEX TASKS

Sometimes a product manager has so much to do that he can feel at a loss for where to begin. But did you know that ancient Greek philosophers contended with the same problem? A typically complex product management activity is planning the launch of a new product. Once you start to think about what's involved, you realize how many things there are to do, and before each of those tasks is a precursor activity, and so on. Before you know it, you're hyperventilating and incapable of even starting. Strangely, this is very much like a problem explored by a philosopher called Zeno in one of his paradoxes.

The philosopher Zeno lived in the fifth century BCE, an elder contemporary of the more famously inquisitive Socrates. He is famous for his many paradoxes, brain teasing puzzles, one of the most intriguing of which is that known as the paradox of the dichotomy, concerning a runner named Atalanta. To complete a race, Zeno reasoned, Atalanta must first reach the halfway point, but in order to get there, she has to first get to the halfway point of that halfway point (a quarter of the distance), and before that, she has to get halfway there (one-eighth), and so on, for an infinite number of halfway points. This means she has an infinite set of distances to cover, so the question is, can she ever get to the finish line? Zeno was trying to refute the concept that infinite division is the same as infinite extent, and the paradox makes handy work of this, as it's quite clearly possible for Atalanta, and any runner, to finish a race. What makes it relevant here is that the image of Atalanta at the starting line envisaging the race as an infinity of tiny distances to travel speaks to the common feeling we can succumb to of being overwhelmed by large jobs. We often find that a task becomes progressively more complex as we get into the details.

Thankfully for both Atalanta and us, common sense prevails: a runner is clearly able to both start and finish a race; we are clearly able to launch products to market. The trick to coping with this overwhelming feeling is to break up large or complex tasks (such as a product launch) into smaller, more digestible ones. You can then group tasks together by area: sales, marketing, PR, finance, and so on. The next step is to categorize whether you (or someone else) need to complete the task now, next week, or later. This should create a much more manageable to-do list. You can then spend a few minutes each day skimming through the list to see what you need to do that day and ignore the rest. At the beginning of each week, get into the habit of checking whether you need to do the tasks now, next week, or later. This way, you're concerning yourself with a smaller set of immediate tasks rather than worrying about the large number of remaining ones. Before you know it, you'll be finishing the race.

LEARNING NOT TO CRASH AND BURN

Despite how complex the cockpit of an aircraft looks, flying a plane doesn't actually require any particularly superhuman skill or fine motor control. An average airplane will naturally want to fly straight and level unless you force it to do otherwise. (With a helicopter, on the other hand, the pilot is continually engaged in a protracted negotiation to persuade the machine not to hurl itself earthward.) So learning to fly is really an exercise in improving one's organization and time management skills.

You may remember from earlier that the pace of the flight training I underwent with the RAF was intense: we'd learn a technique on the ground, then we'd be expected to demonstrate it in the air right away. And if you messed it up once too often, that would be the end of the training. To spice things up every now and again, rather like Cato jumping out of the closet to surprise-attack Inspector Clouseau in the *Pink Panther* movies, my instructor would unexpectedly throw a simulated emergency at me, ranging from the inconvenient (radio failure) to the downright troublesome (engine failure). As I became more experienced, he would present combinations of emergencies to test my ability to prioritize my responses.

Now, I certainly wasn't expected to remember all the details my instructor taught me at once from day one—my head would have caught on fire. Instead, the program built up my skills over time, like building blocks. In the beginning, the focus was on remembering all the external checks on the ground without having to use the reference cards as a prompt. Then I learned to carry out the takeoffs and landings. A little while later I took on responsibility for the radio calls from my instructor, and so on. The key to learning was to repeat new skills in order to commit them to memory, then build more skills on top. The encouraging news is that, over time, by practicing skills this way and consolidating them into memory rapidly, you actually learn *how to learn* more quickly.

On several occasions, the workload of carrying out all the routine flying tasks combined with the new skill we were learning would overwhelm me completely, and I'd experience what I can only describe as a cognitive crash—the human equivalent of Apple's infamous Spinning Beach Ball of Death (which, in case you haven't seen it, is a rainbow-colored pinwheel programmed into the Mac OSX system that appears on-screen to indicate that an application is not responding. It's also referred to as the Marble of Doom). At that point, all bets were off. At best I'd just about be able to continue to fly in a straight line. I'd lose track of where we were, forget all the routine health checks on the aircraft, miss radio calls, and make a real mess of whatever skill we were attempting to learn. In these situations, I'd often find myself fixated on looking out of the cockpit at the pretty, fluffy clouds around us, lost in my own little daydream. It was a weird, light-headed feeling of being both calm and slightly panicked at the same time.

This overload experience was part of the training process. My instructor was deliberately pushing me beyond my cognitive limits so that he could teach me the skill of how to recover from being overwhelmed. Because at some point, it would happen when I'd be flying up there on my own, and I'd have to be the one to drag myself back to normal. And with practice I did become better at coping, which means you certainly can, too.

ONE BRAIN, THREE SPEEDS

So how can you learn to recover from that feeling of being overwhelmed? To do so, it's helpful to understand a little about how we learn skills and how our attention works.

You're probably already familiar with the two systems of decision-making introduced by Daniel Kahneman in *Thinking, Fast and Slow*: our fast, intuitive system and our slow, analytical system. Our fast system responds quickly but sometimes jumps to the wrong conclusions, like when we leap back from a pepper hidden behind leaves in the garden that we mistook for a massive spider. (Just me, then?) Where our fast system makes snap decisions, our slow system brings logic and reasoning into the mix but kicks in only when needed, as it would if I asked you to count the number of commas on this page. What you may not be familiar with is the work of neural networks expert Stuart Dreyfus, who builds on this idea and suggests that there is also a further system for decision-making that is *even faster*.[5] This system provides expert intuition—what we sometimes think of as the "muscle memory" we achieve when we master a skill. An experienced snowboarder like Lucie McLean is using this muscle memory when she doesn't have to think about carving sweeping turns down the slope but just *turns*, and a skilled musician is using it when he doesn't think about playing his instrument but just *plays*. In summary: our muscle memory just *does*, our fast system *reacts*, and our slow system gets out its metaphorical pencil and *works it out*.

When we learn an entirely new skill, at first we have to think quite hard about it. We have to employ our slow system to figure out how we go about doing the task for the first time, even to the point of figuring out which muscles we need to use in which order and which combination to achieve the desired effect. If, for example, you normally play tennis with your right hand, try playing with your left hand instead. To begin with, it will be tremendously difficult, just like you're a complete beginner again. Your arm muscles and hand-eye coordination will be untrained and out of whack, so you'll be lucky if your racket makes contact with anything other than thin air. Your brow will be furrowed and you'll be exerting lots of mental effort to attempt to hit the ball—you'll be predominantly using your slow, analytical system. But then, after a while, something interesting will start to happen. Your brain will realize that what you're trying to do is familiar. Swinging a tennis racket and hitting a ball with your left hand is actually pretty similar to doing it with your right hand, so if you stop thinking about it, you'll probably instinctively start to hit the ball cleanly, if a little weakly. This happens because *without thinking*, your faster, reactive system is able to apply its intuition to help you hit the ball. Eventually the skill will lock in, and you'll then be able to switch your racket effortlessly between your right and left hands.

As you become skilled in a task, its demand for energy diminishes. Studies of the brain have shown that the pattern of activity associated with an action changes as skill increases, with fewer brain regions involved. Talent has similar effects.[6]

So how long does it take to achieve mastery of a skill? In his book *Outliers*, Malcolm Gladwell popularized a (somewhat arbitrary) rule that it generally takes ten thousand hours—or about twenty hours of practice per week for ten years—to become not just proficient but an expert at a cognitively demanding task. There's a good reason why this takes so long: practice makes perfect. Or rather, practice makes myelin. When we perform a task, a pattern of electrical signals is passed down a chain of nerve cells, neuron to neuron, until the signal reaches its destination. The clever part is that if we perform the same tasks repeatedly, the cell grows thicker coats of myelin, a fatty substance that turboboosts the transmission of the electrical signals running through the neurons. This means that the more you practice hitting tennis balls with the racket in your left hand, the quicker and stronger the signals become between your brain and left hand.

In the case of my flight training, each new skill I learned through repetition gradually moved from my slow-thinking system, through my reactive system, and eventually to my muscle memory as my nerve pathways accrued a thicker, glossier coat of myelin. This resulting improvement in the strength and speed of the electrical signals in turn reduced the respective cognitive load of each task, allowing me to perform more of them together. And when I experienced my occasional cognitive crashes, this was because the combination of new and existing flying skills I was actively using had not yet moved from my slow-thinking system. Under pressure, I effectively ran out of brain—the cognitive load required to perform all these tasks exceeded my available capacity—so my mind shut itself down for a short while to cool off. But with more practice of the newly learned skills, I was able to reduce their overall cognitive load and so continue to build up new skills without always becoming overwhelmed at the same point.

In exactly the same way, if you find yourself in overwhelming situations, once you've had a chance to cool down, assess which tasks you found most difficult and practice doing fewer of them at the same time. Doing so will allow them to move from your slow system into the faster thinking systems, thereby reducing their cognitive load. If one of those tasks is the kind of analytical activity that always has to be thought about the slow way, make sure you free up capacity by not attempting other cognitively demanding tasks at the same time. You need to know your limits, but also be aware that repetition gives you the power to make profoundly better use of your cognitive capacity—you'll be genuinely surprised at how efficient you can become with practice.

It's also worth bearing in mind that our brains are not actually very good at multitasking. People who claim to be more efficient through multitasking are deluding themselves. Research has suggested that, at most, our brains can cope with two *concurrent* tasks by splitting them between the two frontal lobes of the brain.[7] Attempting to perform a third task concurrently results in a much higher rate of mistakes.

Here are some examples:

In a 2009 study, Stanford researcher Clifford Nass challenged 262 college students to complete experiments that involved switching among tasks, filtering irrelevant information, and using working memory. Nass and his colleagues expected that frequent multitaskers would outperform nonmultitaskers on at least some of these activities. They found the opposite: chronic multitaskers were abysmal at all three tasks. The scariest part: Only one of the experiments actually involved multitasking, signaling to Nass that even when they focus on a single activity, frequent multitaskers use their brains less effectively.[8]

While individuals who multitask may feel they are getting more done, the reality can be quite different. Participants in a University of Michigan study who were asked to write a report and check e-mail at the same time took one and a half times longer to finish than individuals who did the same two tasks sequentially.[9]

We're far more adept at performing multiple tasks one after another. My own experience bears this out: even when flying, I was only ever really doing two things at once: controlling the plane and one other task, whether it was checking instruments, answering a radio call, or something else. The process of flying as I was taught it is actually an efficiently ordered stream of sequential—not concurrent—activities.

THE FEAR OF MISSING OUT

Is there anyone left who hasn't become addicted to receiving messages? These days our lives are a barrage of little attention-seeking stimuli. Whether it's the melodic chirp of your phone announcing a new text message, the visual notification of a new email arriving on your laptop, or the flashing of the LED on the coffee machine to tell you it's busy creating your fresh, fragrant brew, it draws your attention away, even if only for a second or two.

Each one of these little attention-grabbing cues triggers a release of noradrenaline in our brains, which in turn causes our perception and thinking to become more alert and ready for what's about to come. We receive a pleasing little burst of excitement and anticipation (a mini-reward in itself) that, when combined with the gratification of reading the new text message or email or drinking the freshly brewed coffee, makes the whole experience habit forming. In a study of our information habits published in 2011, Dr. Martin Hilbert determined that people were processing an astonishing five times more information in 2007 than in 1986 as a result of the digital revolution and the rise of social media.[10] Imperceptibly, over the years, we've grown accustomed to an increasing level of stimulation, so that today we operate normally in a much higher state of sensory arousal than we have done in the past. The good news is that our brains are plastic enough to adapt to this change in pace and have the capacity to continue adapting. However, we also have to consider the effect this is having on our attention. The technologies that cater to our heightened craving for sensory stimulation—social media; mobile devices; or, more intrusive, interactive advertising—are extremely effective at holding our rapt attention.

Combined with this heightened level of sensory stimulation is the psychological phenomenon known as the fear of missing out. Some of us are disproportionately worried by what might happen if we fail to read the juicy bit of gossip or see the hysterical cat video the next email or tweet may have in store. Psychiatrist John Grohol, an expert on online behavior and the author of the PsychCentral blog, astutely observes:

> We are so connected with one another through our Twitter streams and Foursquare check-ins, through our Facebook and LinkedIn updates, that we can't just be alone anymore. The fear of missing out (FOMO)—on something more fun, on a social date that might just happen on the spur of the moment—is so intense, even when we've decided to disconnect, we still connect just once more, just to make sure.[11]

Despite our newly acquired ability to process many times more information than before, we're simply more easily distracted than we used to be. This increased competition for our attention and our apparent inability to concentrate for long make time management skills all the more important for everyone, not just product managers.

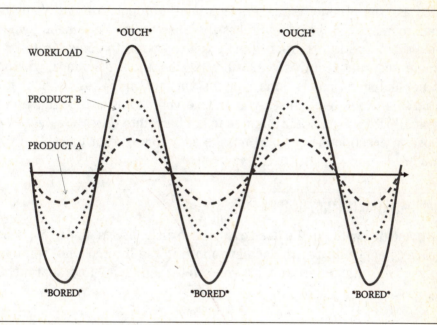

No matter how you plan it, product workloads always seem to stack up. (Courtesy of Jock Busuttil)

The workload intensity of product managers tends to be cyclical, and sometimes these cycles can stack up. When you're busy, distractions can seriously dent your ability to Get Stuff Done™. Yet everyone seems to want a piece of a product manager. I don't know whether it's due to our natural charisma or simply because we're helpful people and happen to know pretty much everything about our products (sadly, in my case I suspect it's only the latter). Be aware that people soon figure out that the quickest way to answer a product question is to ask the product manager. This is often a good thing—it's better that someone ask you than guess the answer or ask someone who'll give them bad information. But if you're trying to concentrate on a single task that requires your full attention, these questions, whether in person or via phone, email, or instant messaging, are serious distractions. Each one causes you to lose your train of thought, and it typically takes you a few minutes to get back into the groove. A few of those interruptions per hour and it's easy to see what a problem this can be.

WORKING SMARTER, NOT HARDER

To avoid drowning in the flood of all these distractions, find some headspace to concentrate, and achieve more in the limited time you have to work, I'd like to share with you a few techniques and approaches I've used.

Disable Notifications

When you're up against a deadline and need to maintain your focus on the task at hand, you absolutely must close down your email and instant messaging. If you don't, you'll find it almost impossible to resist the urge to check them, especially if they have attention-grabbing notifications. The only way to break the habit of checking is to remove the cue to do so. By the same token, divert all calls to voice mail, and switch off your smartphone (they do have an "Off" button; I've checked) or sling it into your desk drawer where you can't see or hear it. If you can't do that for some reason, turn the volume of the ringer down (or, ideally, off). For landlines, unplug. I'm serious. The vast majority of calls are not about something urgent. If the matter is pressing, the caller will simply find someone else to help them out, usually the person they probably should have been calling to begin with—you don't have to facilitate every product discussion in your company. It would, however, be unwise to unplug at key junctures when you know you'll probably be urgently needed, such as on launch day.

Be Elsewhere

If you've used the previous technique a few times too often, your colleagues will learn to come and find you at your desk. The queues will start to form and any chance of meeting that deadline goes back out the window. This is when it's important to deploy your second technique of being elsewhere. Aside from the positive effect of a lovely change of scenery, working from a different part of the office or at home makes it much more difficult for people to come by and disturb you. I've also found this is a great opportunity to get to know people from other departments better, which in turn makes it easier to ask for a favor later on. Needless to say, you can't hide away too often, but now and then it affords you the necessary headspace to prevent overload and allow you to focus on the biggest fires.

Note Down Distractions

If you're like me, a distraction can set you off thinking about something more interesting than your primary task. Keep a notepad by your desk, and every time your mind wanders to something other than the job at hand, write it down for later. This can greatly reduce your cognitive load. Similarly, when someone comes to your desk asking you to do something, even if it's potentially quick, visibly take a note down and be clear that you first need to finish the task you're working on. You may find you have to stand your ground occasionally, as some people will insist you do what they've requested immediately.

(Re)take Control of Your Schedule

In some companies, everyone's online calendar is a free-for-all (or at least, everyone who's not a senior manager). Everyone has permission to view, create, and edit entries in anyone else's calendar. This places you at the mercy of invitations to innumerable pointless meetings. By fiddling around with the settings for your online calendar, you can usually control who has permission to book you into meetings and how much detail people can see of your schedule. Frankly, all I generally want people to know is whether I'm busy or free. Everything else is on a need-to-know basis. Making this change will mean you can start to block out uninterrupted time in your calendar for your own tasks.

Use the Four *D*s of Email

Product managers just loooove solving problems and answering questions. Emails present us with an enticing list of both, which is yet another reason we find it so hard to tear ourselves away from them. The trick to regaining control over your emails is to skim them and use the Four *D*s: *Delete, Defer, Delegate,* and *Do.*

The proportion of emails in each category typically decrease from Delete through to Do, roughly corresponding to the size of the semicircles in the figure. This will result in the number of emails you need to respond to immediately being quite minimal.

You should devote regular slots of time in your schedule to the tasks that are a constant part of your work, such as reading and responding to emails, to prevent these tasks from being constant interruptions. The trick is then to be sufficiently self-disciplined to ensure that you use the allotted time—and no more—for each specific task. It may be

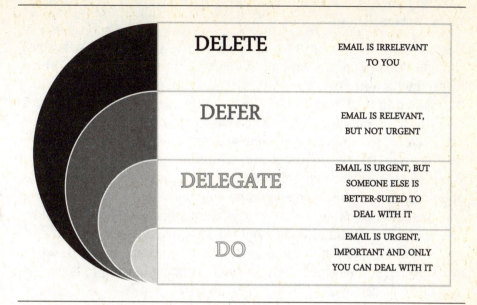

DELETE	EMAIL IS IRRELEVANT TO YOU
DEFER	EMAIL IS RELEVANT, BUT NOT URGENT
DELEGATE	EMAIL IS URGENT, BUT SOMEONE ELSE IS BETTER-SUITED TO DEAL WITH IT
DO	EMAIL IS URGENT, IMPORTANT AND ONLY YOU CAN DEAL WITH IT

The four Ds of email (Courtesy of Jock Busuttil)

difficult to do at first, but after a few days you'll find it becomes easier to be disciplined. This technique has the added benefit of training other people to know and respect your routine.

Have a "No Meetings" Day Each Week

Striking all meetings from a single day may sound impossible, but think of it this way: when you're on vacation you don't attend meetings, and yet the business still manages without you, so it's clearly not impossible. If you really can't deflect all those meeting requests, fake some vacation time in your calendar, then be elsewhere. It's a good idea to tell your manager you're doing this, but reassure her that you'll get far more done this way. Then you can concentrate on all your work in peace.

Work Normal Hours

Part of managing your time involves giving your colleagues a reasonable perception of how long it takes to do things. Even if you're
blessed with a great work ethic, snatching an extra hour or seven by
turning up to work early, staying late, or working on the weekends is
cheating (and counterproductive), regardless of how much you think
you need to. Not only do you wear yourself down when you should be
having some time to yourself and with your friends and family, but
you also set an unrealistically high expectation with your colleagues
about how much work you should be able to do from week to week. If
you then stop working extra hours, guess what? You'll start looking
like you're not trying as hard. So it's best to avoid that by working the
hours you're supposed to. If you can't get everything done in the time
available, everyone (including yourself) is going to have to learn that
more time is needed.

Stop Doing Things

One of the easiest ways to spot a product manager in the wild is to
look for the slightly frazzled person with a long to-do list and a determined, though perhaps somewhat crazed, look in their eye. Although
I think we generally enjoy keeping ourselves busy, I've often noticed
over a beer with colleagues that we (myself included) also quite enjoy
moaning about how much there is to do and that the work is never-
ending. It's usually second on the conversational agenda, just after
the obligatory "Isn't sales exasperating?" mantra.

My to-do list tends to break down into three categories of tasks:

1. Things I have to do right now, and ideally yesterday
2. Things I need to do as part of "business as usual"
3. All the other things I would love to have a chance to do if time
   permitted

Because we product managers are generally motivated, diligent types, there's always a heap of things in that third, wish list category that we'd like to do if we had the time. So in some respects, we've got only ourselves to blame for our to-do lists being so long. If the overall length of your list is what's been stressing you out, think about how many of those tasks you actually need to do.

One approach to tackling this (with the blessing of your manager) is simply to stop doing a selection of the ever-present "business as usual" tasks for a month and see if anybody notices. These kinds of tasks might include a selection of performance reports you've been diligently compiling each month (or week) for senior management. The chances are that nobody will notice, which usually means those tasks are no longer necessary, so you can probably ditch most of them. This will free you up to tackle a few more items on your wish list.

I ALMOST NEVER GOT AROUND TO WRITING THIS SECTION ON PROCRASTINATION

It's a small miracle you're reading this book.

Procrastination is one of the most common, and most corrosive, problems in personal time management. For me, one of the typical ways I procrastinate is to find all sorts of other, not truly pressing things I could do. These are often useful tasks but not particularly urgent, and certainly of much lower importance than what I'm supposed to be doing. However, they tend to be activities where I have a clear idea of where to start, how to do them, and what "finished" looks like. Lovely Wife called me out on this the other day when I described how I'd finally gotten around to carting a pile of stuff to the nearby recycling facility—a pile that I'd been perfectly happy to allow to gather dust for months prior to starting to write this book. The certainty of the alternate activity and its completion is a reassurance, a security blanket, with the bonus feeling of having done something faintly useful. It's essentially a displaced reward: "I may not have done the one thing I was supposed to do today, but I've done all these other things instead. That must count for something, right?"

The good news is that most of us are aware when we're beginning to procrastinate. I know I always recognize that there's something important I need to do and that I'm allowing myself to be distracted. This makes training ourselves out of the practice eminently doable. I've used a few simple techniques. The first is the commonly used method, always worth mentioning, of keeping a written list of the most important things to do in order of urgency. My second and possibly more powerful tactic is to preempt an incipient bout of procrastination by removing the sources of distraction. I've covered a number of ways to do so earlier in this chapter. Discipline yourself about these strategies, and you will find over time that you are less inclined to engage in procrastination. Protecting yourself from interruptions and from cognitive load really helps you feel more energized to get on with tackling bigger tasks.

The trick is to recognize your personal triggers for procrastination. For me, it's usually the feeling of discomfort and anxiety about a difficult or important task ahead that sets me off. A way I've effectively tackled this is to turn what looks in my mind like an uncertain, open-ended activity into one that is more certain and has a better-defined start and finish. This is where the tactic of dividing up a large, complex, and uncertain project into lots of smaller, simpler, and more easily defined tasks is especially helpful. As previously mentioned, the increasingly popular Agile development process Scrum is premised on exactly this tactic: it breaks down large, complex product requirements (called "epics") into smaller, bite-sized ones (called "user stories"). Not only does this make tracking progress easier and more continuous, so big problems don't emerge all of a sudden toward the end, but it makes the job of developing the project a good deal less daunting overall. Rather than attempting to research and define the entire product up front and build it over the course of years (during which time the market needs move on), only to watch it fail at release because it no longer solves the market problem, Scrum allows the team to make course corrections as they go to take into account new information learned. If you aren't familiar with it, you will definitely want to be. And you can incorporate the same philosophy into your own working methods easily. You'll see that if you break down your own complex tasks into more manageable, bite-sized chunks, you will not be as anxious at the start about how you're going to get the job done and will feel less uncertainty mounting along the way about how things will turn out. In addition, by working in this way, you'll experience a little rush of achievement for each piece completed. Over time, this is a way to harness the mechanisms of addiction for the cause of productivity.

Projects that threaten to overwhelm you are always going to come along; that will remain true no matter how long you've been a product manager. Snafus are simply a part of the product development business, and no management process is ever going to be able to do away with them all. But by making use of these simple techniques for focusing your attention and getting a tighter grip on your time, you'll be able to keep the plane aloft no matter what surprises come flying at you.

POINTS TO REMEMBER

Tender Loving Care of Time

» You need to be able to divide your attention between the concerns of the here-and-now and what's looming on the horizon.
» With practice, even the most terminally disorganized person can learn to organize herself.
» Everyone will run out of brain eventually. Avoid becoming overwhelmed by practicing unfamiliar tasks to reduce their cognitive load.

(continued)

» Managing sources of distraction is the key to unlocking more efficient ways of working.
» Think about whether tasks on your to-do list are urgent and important.
» Taking time to absorb more information improves the quality of your decision; avoid making decisions as a knee-jerk reaction.
» Deadlines help motivate you to complete important tasks. Promise someone that you'll have the work ready for them, then don't let them down.
» Make complex tasks more manageable by breaking them down into smaller pieces and determining whether you or someone else is best placed to do them.

CONCLUSION

Grab a pen and a piece of paper. What do you now think constitutes success as a product manager? Write down the first thing that comes into your mind. It's okay—I'll hang on until you're done.

What did you write?

Many product managers would write, "Success is my product hitting its targets," and that's a reasonable place to start. But is it fair to judge a product manager solely on the success of his or her product? How else can you judge whether you're doing your job well? Depending on your personal motivations, you may want to know for your own satisfaction, to give your boss evidence at your next pay review, or to give your résumé some teeth for your next job. As we've explored, there are some things in your working life that you can control directly, some you can't, and some you can influence. Because product management is mostly an influencing role (we're generalists who rely on specialists to make the product successful), the problem with the traditional key performance indicators that companies use for product managers is that they often focus only on the performance of the *products*, not the *people*. There are, however, some better alternatives for measuring how successful you are.

You could argue that the good financial performance and high customer satisfaction of your products are reasonable indicators of good product manager performance. The problem with using the product as a proxy is that product managers are generally one step removed from both of these measures. Let me try to explain why. We don't sell the product. Okay, we do sometimes, but that's not the day job.

And assuming for a second that customer satisfaction is primarily a result of good product design, similarly we're not (meant to be) designing the product, just specifying the problems for the designers to go away and solve creatively. Again, we're not *directly* affecting customer satisfaction. Even if we perform every aspect of our product management responsibilities to a high standard, we can't necessarily guarantee that everyone else involved will. So we need other ways of measuring how well we do our jobs.

One approach would be to gauge your performance by asking the people with whom you regularly interact for feedback on how you're doing—like the "How's my driving?" signs on the backs of trucks. To the development team, you might ask: How easy were my requirements to understand? To marketing: How well did I explain what would be in the forthcoming release? To the sales team: How much additional commission have I gifted you this month? Perhaps you can see where I'm going with this. It's seemingly a short hop before we end up bribing everyone we speak to with a chance to win an iPad to get them to complete a short survey on how satisfied they were with the content of our conversation. I can't see that working in the long run; can you? There is also a trend toward so-called 360-degree performance appraisals that essentially take this very approach. Such reviews are arguably flawed because they rely on the people giving the feedback to be completely objective, rather than take the opportunity to either do a favor for their drinking buddies or exact revenge for some perceived past slight. At what point did corporate performance appraisals become a popularity contest? Instead, let's try a different tack by measuring our success by the outcomes of the activities we can control directly, such as the market research, roadmapping, product launches, and decommissioning activities we explored in more detail earlier.

Product managers undertake many different tasks with both long- and short-term goals, but what we're aiming for is quality, not necessarily quantity. Assuming we're doing the right tasks to begin with, if we can do them well (and objectively measure that we are doing so), then successful products will naturally result.

REASONS NOT TO BECOME A PRODUCT MANAGER

Like twerking and selfies,[1] product management has for some reason recently undergone a transition, from being a practice understood by few except its immediate practitioners and employed at a few companies to being a practice understood by few except its immediate practitioners but *in much greater demand.* I'm not complaining about this change in attitude in itself, but accompanying it is a slew of people who reckon they can become product managers simply because they happen to have used products a few times.

"I want to create the best possible products."

Some people want to become product managers because they want to build the best possible products. To those people: I commend your noble mission, but you've sure as hell got your work cut out for you. There seem to be few entirely satisfying products out there. Other than a hi-fi amplifier I bought on the cheap in 1996 with the money I'd made from inexpertly decorating my brother's flat,* I have very few products on my shortlist of Best Products Ever. Everything else has been a bit mediocre in one way or another.

Job interviews used to particularly wind me up. Having looked up the big, big book of clever questions for prospective product managers, the interviewer would say, "Tell me about how you'd improve our product." And I'd have to suppress the urge to tell them that I would improve their product by taking it round the back with my metaphorical shotgun in order to put it out of its misery; that I'd replace it with

---

* A Denon DRA-275RD, if you must know. I've never successfully turned the volume dial up beyond a third without bursting an eardrum.

something people actually wanted to use, rather than were forced to because there were no practical alternatives available or because swapping it out would be too expensive and effortful. (I didn't receive many job offers for some time.)

So don't become a product manager because you expect that you'll be responsible for creating the best, most loved products in the world. At some point the planets may align and you may have the opportunity and the presence of mind to do that, but for the most part you'll be dealing with an imperfect, mediocre product in an organization that doesn't like to be told that its baby is ugly. On the positive side, at least you'll understand and sympathize with the customers who gather each evening outside your office window with pitchforks and burning torches.

"I want control over product strategy."

Some people go into product management because they seek POWER. They think they'll waft in and wield the magic say-so on how to quadruple product sales. Everything will suddenly be peachy; there'll be some kind of ticker-tape parade and possibly cake. The bitter pill here is that it doesn't work like that. At all. Product strategies that work perfectly in your own head rarely follow the same script in the real world—particularly when other people get involved.

The fly in your dictatorial ointment is that a product manager rarely wields true authority. Even if you have other product managers, business analysts, or even developers in your charge, everyone else in the company will be quite content to continue as they are without your interference, thank you. Your efficacy as a product manager is only as good as your ability to influence and persuade others to follow your plan. If you want to become a product manager because you want to run the show unchallenged and unfettered by the need to persuade people to do things differently, now would be a great time to reevaluate your career path. Have you considered a role in senior management?

One Further Thought

If you harbor some misguided fantasy that your career in product management will be something about which your parents can brag to their friends over coffee, bridge, or gin, please understand that your parents will NEVER understand what you do. To them, you'll always be "doing something in computers." You'll still be obliged on every visit home to fix their laptops, Wi-Fi, printers, cameras, and any other electronic device created after they had kids.* If you're looking for professional recognition from your parents, you may wish to consider becoming a lawyer, doctor, priest, or light entertainment game show host instead.

Still here? Good.

If you were considering a career in product management and all this hasn't put you off, well done! You're probably tenacious (read: stubborn) enough to deal with days on which every step forward is immediately followed by two steps back and with the frustration of senior executives derailing your carefully researched product strategy in favor of something they thought up in the shower that morning. These are the Herculean labors through which you'll have to fight your way in order to reach and savor those brief, glistening moments of whooping, air-punching triumph of a product done well. There's no other experience quite like it, and I wouldn't have it any other way.

MOVING INTO PRODUCT MANAGEMENT

One of the questions people ask me most often is what they need to do to become a product manager. So here are some of the practicalities. As I found when making the leap from product marketing to product management, changing job titles can be tricky at the best of times,

---

* It is a documented medical fact (not really) that the part of the brain that permits the understanding of new technologies shuts down on the occasion of the birth of one's first child.

more so if you find yourself stuck in the chicken-and-egg conundrum of needing experience to secure your first job in a new area. You also may not have the freedom to move between roles in your current organization, which may well mean that you're going to need to seek this experience elsewhere. One good way to get that experience is by doing an internship. Another is to move into a stepping-stone job, of which there are several that are particularly good routes in. As a rough guideline—by no means an exhaustive list—these are all job titles you could look for to gain experience in each of the three rings I introduced in the first chapter:

» **User experience:** product marketer; market analyst; competitive analyst; technical support; usability tester; user interaction, visual, or user experience designer
» **Business:** business insight or business intelligence analyst, account manager, roles in client services and business development
» **Technology:** technical support, business analyst, requirements engineer, web designer or developer, project manager, developer or engineer, operations

Taking an incremental approach to building up your experience in each of these three main areas has additional benefits. Remember, you don't really know for sure at this stage whether product management is for you, so you'll be much better placed to decide whether you enjoy it by dipping your toe in, rather than plunging in and struggling to keep your head above water. Building up your skills over time also allows them to settle in and become second nature by the time you need to bring them all together for your first role in product management. It took me six years after university to find my first product manager job, though admittedly part of that time was spent discovering product management in the first place.

My first job as a product manager was at Iron Mountain, a company better known for the storage of physical data—literally millions of boxes of paper in just *one* of their thousands of warehouses—than for software. It was formerly known as the Iron Mountain Atomic Storage Corporation, founded by a chap called Herman Knaust, who decided there was better money to be made from storing corporate papers in his old iron ore mine than from growing mushrooms. (It presumably would also have been comforting to know that come the nuclear apocalypse, the nation's biggest hoard of contracts, invoices, and meeting minutes would be tucked up safe and sound, while everyone aboveground had been turned to ash.) As part of my interview, I was asked to give a presentation on what product management was. It soon became clear that it was as new a discipline to the company as it was to me. Given the way general awareness of the discipline has progressed since then, I think it would be advisable to spend three to four years building up your skills in preparation—and probably fewer if you're starting out with a slightly more relevant degree than I did with classics.

You'll tend to find that younger, smaller companies and startups are more familiar with product management, and so this is where you'll likely find many of the jobs being advertised. Becoming the product manager at a startup places an even bigger burden on your shoulders than usual. Think of the cofounders' emotional rollercoaster; all their long, poorly paid days of toil to reach this point. All that time spent living and breathing their product, nurturing it, dealing with its faults and civilizing it into a viable business. All those dreams, disagreements, and decisions about its future; all the hopes they've fostered of seeing it become the Next Big Thing. All the money they've personally invested to get here. Now they entrust all of this to you. You do not want to screw it up.

It is also perfectly possible that you'll join a larger corporation that recognizes that product managers will somehow improve its success but has little concept of the remit and extent of their role. As I found at Iron Mountain, it can be a tall order to educate your company on best practice while you're still learning about it yourself. Joining any company as a product manager is a hefty responsibility; small, medium, and large companies each have their own distinctive challenges.

Smaller companies are more intimate and relaxed in some respects but can be chaotic while the company's still finding its niche. Expect to get good at acquiring new skills quickly. "Adolescent" companies have more stability, but the cultural changes that often accompany the transition to a more mature operation can cause a lot of upheaval. And it can be equally hard to effect change in larger companies that are geared toward sustaining the status quo rather than innovating on it. It's still worthwhile to experience all three, however.

Another way into the profession is to apply for a product management role internally or push to create one in your current organization. This can be a simpler process in some respects—after all, you know the company and products, and they know you—but it may take longer than applying for jobs elsewhere. Even if you do a great job of convincing the powers that be of the need for the role, its potential benefits, and your suitability, they will need to rearrange staff budgets, team structures, and all that jazz to make the change happen. They'll also potentially need to recruit someone to backfill the gap you've created. Be concerned if they don't; either they're saying they don't see the need for that role, affording you no way back if the new position doesn't work out, or they're expecting you to take on the product management responsibilities *in addition* to whatever you were doing before. (That can be fun.) Politics may come into this process as well, particularly if the creation of a new role upsets the balance of power between department heads, though this will likely happen "above your pay grade," as the cliché goes.

The downside of applying for an internal role is that it will be clear that you're looking for a change. If you're rebuffed, whether because of your employer's lack of desire, lack of budget, or even *Game of Thrones*-esque politicking, you may also be a bit miffed that it didn't work out. To this I say: get over yourself—product managers have to deal with setbacks all the time. Use your product manager superpowers to figure out another way around the problem, just as you would with anything else. In management terms, however, you may now be considered a "flight risk": someone with a greater likelihood of leaving the organization altogether. For balance, it doesn't always have to turn out this way. If you, your manager, and your organization have an open and mature approach to employee development and performance management, and if you genuinely enjoy working where you are, don't throw a good job away. (I apologize for sounding like your parents.) There's every chance you can establish why it didn't work out this time, allowing you and your manager to remove the obstacles and in effect create your career roadmap by setting out what specifically you need to do in order to achieve the promotion to product manager.

Some people dream of working for a specific company they particularly admire. Unfortunately there's no guarantee that a position will conveniently open up. Going out into the world and creating your ideal role by convincing a company that it needs you isn't as impossible as it sounds. It will, however, require a bit more investment of time and effort on your part. In effect, you're identifying an unsatisfied need for a product manager in a niche market of organizations that you'd like to work for. This should sound familiar. So given that you're now the product, the solution to your target's unmet need for a product manager, think about how you can help the organization to see the need you've identified, then connect that with your benefits (the real-world, positive effect you'll have) and your features (the combination of your experience and skills). Think about your unique selling points and your unfair advantages, show your understanding of the problems you can solve for the organization, and be able to articulate them. As with any other market problem you encounter, bear in mind that the customer may not be aware of the need you've identified, so you may need to reveal it to them gently and diplomatically.

A variant on this approach is to strike out on your own as a freelancer, a route I've taken. I'd been working at Experian for several years when it dawned on me that I'd been doing product management in a particular way at the same place for a while, and although I was reasonably successful at it, I felt that I was going through the motions without really learning anything new. Because I was a senior team manager, opportunities to move up were infrequent and unpredictable, and sideways moves to other departments didn't look very appealing. It was also becoming clear to me that I wanted the opportunity to balance my hands-on product management with a bit more writing and teaching and that I needed to build up and vary my experience by working for startups and in more consumer-focused companies. Leaving the company also gave me the joyous opportunity to slip into the customary good-bye email to the company that I was off to continue writing under my pen name, E. L. James, mainly to see who was paying attention.

When I left, I didn't initially plan to start freelancing, but it turned out that the work suited my needs well. As an added bonus, I now appreciate much more the benefits of working with specialists in marketing, client care, finance, and other disciplines, since I've had to manage the whole kit and caboodle of running a business single-handedly. There have been highs and lows along the way: successfully closing my first client; realizing I was underselling myself by about half; running user interviews in Rwanda; and having the opportunity to work with talented developers and designers, some of whom have since gone on to work at Apple and Facebook. And I've been able to blend all this with some teaching and writing—hence this book. Gin and tonics all around.

I should also stress that the freelancing option is not for everyone. I count myself particularly lucky that I've been able to find a steady and timely stream of clients thus far. Lovely Wife had only given me carte blanche to run the freelancing experiment for a year, so if by that point I hadn't garnered any meaningful business, I suspect her patience would have worn thin and she'd have kicked my sorry ass out the door to seek gainful employment once more. If you do go the freelancing route, set yourself some realistic objectives and a time limit so you know when to cut your losses, dust off your résumé, and get a haircut.

WHAT WILL THEY SAY AT YOUR GOOD-BYE SPEECH?

I remember when a good friend and colleague left the company at which we both worked to take on a more senior product management role elsewhere. His boss and his boss's boss stood next to him and gave him a glowing and sincere send-off, striking that lovely balance between "We're sad to see you leave" and "Go out, excel, and make us proud." So much of being a product manager boils down to how we conduct ourselves and how we relate to others. Even if your product becomes a runaway success, you'll still be remembered unfavorably if you got there by annoying everyone on the way. By the same token, "nice guy, but completely ineffectual" would not be such a great legacy, either. Think about how others will respond to the way you act and how you can go about your task of achieving success for your products with integrity, good humor, and purpose. This is what will determine how people will remember you.

Success means something different to everyone. Over the years, I've had the good fortune to meet and work with many inspirational product managers. Here are a few of their stories so you can see what success means to them.

Paul Malyon

I fell into product management somewhat by accident after looking after a CRM system and associated database for a few years. I guess the fact I was working for a startup and dabbled in a bit of everything helped prepare me for the variety of tasks I'd need to tackle as a product manager.

I've progressed relatively quickly up the ladder over the past three years from a junior role to a couple of team leader positions, where I'm now responsible for a few successful product lines and the future strategy of these within a large multinational. My proudest product launch was that of a major new location-based set of reference data for the UK public sector. By reacting quickly and understanding the customer needs, I was able to position myself as a thought leader and my product as market-leading. This led to me being asked to represent my industry on a government advisory body and influenced my move upward to a new role within my company.

(continued)

Janna Bastow

I became a product manager by accident. I used to want to be a product packaging designer—you know, designing the foldy boxes or bottles and whatnot that stuff comes in. While working at a small graphic design studio, I realized I'm not as much of a pure artist as I might have hoped, and that I knew even less about actually running a studio or any other small business. So instead I took an e-business course at college, learning about things like how eBay and Amazon make money and what this Friendster thing is. One class was on project management, which seemed interesting enough, so for a while I was enamored with getting the PMP (project management professional) certification.

When I left college, I took a job as a support/account rep at a tech company. The development team quickly realized that I was halfway decent at reporting bugs and outlining requested changes, and they plucked me out of support and made me a junior product manager. "I like the way you call bullshit when you see it," my boss told me as he promoted me. But I'd been gunning for a project management role—I'd never heard of product management, so I had to Google it when I'd gotten back to my desk.

[My biggest] success? Erm...tough one; I guess going from square one, where I had to hunt for product management tools (my second most important Google query that day), to building my own and selling them to other product managers. I particularly love hearing from my users about how ProdPad's been a teaching mechanism to help them become better product managers. I love that, and I suppose helping people build better products would be my biggest measure of success.

Simon Cast

I've been doing product management from very early on in my career, though usually not as the primary role. I started out as a space engineer and satellite orbital dynamicist for Optus in Australia. While there I happened to be involved in creating various internal products that helped with operations. Around that time I joined the Australian Army to train as a combat engineering officer, which was fantastic for leadership, planning, and management training. Looking back, surprisingly a lot of what I learned was to plan the delivery of a product—though in this case a bridge, a bunker, fortifications, buildings (or destruction of said structure)—and then work with the specialists, the sappers and their NCOs (noncommissioned officers) to deliver that "product."

After leaving the army I moved to the UK, where I landed a role as an analyst for a consultancy. At the time the consultancy was turning its intellectual property into a product, which I took charge of. We achieved Series A funding only to have the financial crisis crunch the next round of funding. I left and joined PeerIndex in its very early stages, finally gaining the official title of product manager for the first time.

Success for me is taking raw, incomplete, and untested ideas all the way through prototype to MVP to product, and eventually to the point where revenue's coming in and the CEO's able to land a Series A funding round. While that's by no means the end of the story, the process of getting the product to a point where people are paying for it is hugely rewarding. It's also been wonderful to build Mind the Product into a global community with Janna and Martin, and to talk to people who have found a community for themselves, a new job, or even an entirely new career as a result.

Earlier in the chapter, I asked you to write down what success meant for you personally, so it's only fair that I do the same. As you've had a chance to read in this book, throughout my life I've thought that success meant making the grade academically, or living the exciting life of a fighter pilot, or working the hardest, or earning a fat salary, or changing the world with my products. And if I'm honest, on these criteria alone, I've achieved only moderate success (so far). However, I think that I've discovered what success *really* means for me: it's waking up each morning and having a sense of happy anticipation about what product management will throw my way that day, and going to bed each night satisfied that I've worked to the standard I expect from myself. It's having the opportunity to work with people whose skill and professionalism I admire and aspire to, and it's the rewarding feeling of acquiring a new skill or knowledge that allows me to view the world from a new perspective.

That, and never having to wear a tie again.

In many ways, I'm very happy that serendipity has led me to become a product manager, but as you'll hopefully appreciate by now, it's not been the most straightforward or easy path to reach this point, as I'm sure is the case for many others. So in parting, I'd like to pass on one more piece of advice I've learned the hard way: **strike the right balance**. It's good to care about your product and invest yourself in it, but the product is not a part of you, and it's certainly not your "baby." If you're losing sleep at night over user stories, presentations, or business cases; habitually working late; and generally not enjoying yourself, try to take a step back and regain a little perspective. Product management is a profession that can chew up people and spit them out again, but it is just a *job*; a means to the end of earning enough money to allow you to do the things that really matter to you a little more easily. When it comes down to it, the most important measure of success is your happiness and contentment. That's the hardest thing I've had to learn on my journey to becoming an expert product manager.

Product management is a dynamic, challenging, and in-demand profession. It encompasses the art, skill, and science of observing a market, forming an idea, and turning it into a successful product. It is an enticing blend of the creative and the analytical, and it is rarely dull. If you picture yourself in ten or fifteen years' time as the CEO of a vast technology corporation—just look at Marissa Mayer, who started out as a product manager at a small startup called Google—then product management is the perfect way to enable you to achieve that. Good luck!

ACKNOWLEDGMENTS

There are several people I need to thank in particular for their assistance in writing this book: Emma Walker, Laura Hasting, Matt Cynamon, and Brad Hargreaves from General Assembly for variously recommending, encouraging, and asking me to write this in the first place; Emily Loose, for all her hard work crafting my manuscript into the finished product you hold today, for helping me become a proper writer, and for spending many hours discussing the similarities between product management and publishing with me; and, in no particular order, Helen Holmes, Martin Eriksson, Janna Bastow, Simon Cast, Alison Austin, Lucie McLean, Vanessa Bruce, Sam Ellenby, Jamie Krisman, Lisa Dowdeswell, Kate Pool, Dermot Wilson, Kate Leto, Gianluca Trombetta, Christopher Lewis, Tom Sadler, Paul Malyon, Adrienne Tan, Mike Atherton, Laura Cherkas, and Cohorts Two and Three from my product management classes at General Assembly, London, for their interest and help in various ways. Thank you all.

I would also like to reserve a special note of thanks for my lovely wife, Jo, for her support, inspiration, and occasional shaming of my daily word count with her own writing.

Jock Busuttil, London,
May 2014

FURTHER READING

Books

Ariely, Dan. *Predictably Irrational: The Hidden Forces That Shape Our Decisions.* New York: Harper Perennial, 2010.

Blanchard, Ken, Patricia Zigarmi, and Drea Zigarmi. *Leadership and the One Minute Manager: Increasing Effectiveness Through Situational Leadership II.* Updated ed. New York: Morrow, 2014.

Blank, Steve. *The Four Steps to the Epiphany: Successful Strategies for Products That Win.* California: S. G. Blank, 2007.

Cagan, Marty. *Inspired: How to Create Products Customers Love.* California: SVPG Press, 2008.

Davidson, Neil. *Don't Just Roll the Dice: A Usefully Short Guide to Software Pricing.* Cambridge, UK: Red Gate, 2009.

Drucker, Peter F. *The Effective Executive: The Definitive Guide to Getting the Right Things Done.* New York: Collins, 2006.

Drucker, Peter F. *The Practice of Management.* New York: Collins, 2006.

Duhigg, Charles. *The Power of Habit: Why We Do What We Do in Life and Business.* New York: Random House, 2012.

Eeles, Tom. *A Passion for Flying: 8,000 Hours of RAF Flying.* Barnsley, UK: Pen & Sword Aviation, 2008.

Gladwell, Malcolm. *Outliers: The Story of Success.* New York: Back Bay Books, 2011.

Haig, Matt. *Brand Failures: The Truth About the 100 Biggest Branding Mistakes of All Time.* 2nd ed. London: Kogan Page, 2011.

Hatch, Mark. *The Maker Movement Manifesto: Rules for Innovation in the New World of Crafters, Hackers, and Tinkerers.* New York: McGraw-Hill Education, 2014.

Isaacson, Walter. *Steve Jobs.* New York: Simon & Schuster, 2011.

Kahneman, Daniel. *Thinking, Fast and Slow.* New York: Farrar, Straus and Giroux, 2013.

Kemper, Steve. *Reinventing the Wheel: A Story of Genius, Innovation, and Grand Ambition*. New York: HarperBusiness, 2005.

Klein, Stefan. *Time: A User's Guide*. London: Penguin Books, 2008.

Moore, Geoffrey A. *Crossing the Chasm: Marketing and Selling Disruptive Products to Mainstream Customers*. 3rd ed. New York: HarperBusiness, 2014.

Olins, Wally. *Brand New: The Shape of Brands to Come*. New York: Thames & Hudson, 2014.

Osterwalder, Alexander, and Yves Pigneur. *Business Model Generation: A Handbook for Visionaries, Game Changers, and Challengers*. Hoboken, NJ: Wiley, 2010.

Partnoy, Frank. *Wait: The Art and Science of Delay*. New York: PublicAffairs, 2012.

Pichler, Roman. *Agile Product Management with Scrum: Creating Products That Customers Love*. Upper Saddle River, NJ: Addison-Wesley, 2010.

Ries, Eric. *The Lean Startup: How Today's Entrepreneurs Use Continuous Innovation to Create Radically Successful Businesses*. New York: Crown Business, 2011.

Blogs

Applied Frameworks Blog, http://appliedframeworks.com/blog/.

Brainrants, http://www.brainmates.com.au/recent-brainrants.

The Cranky Product Manager, http://crankypm.com.

I Manage Products, http://imanageproducts.co.uk.

Joel on Software, http://www.joelonsoftware.com.

Mind the Product, http://www.mindtheproduct.com.

Rich Mironov's Product Bytes, http://www.mironov.com.

Pmarchive, http://pmarchive.com.

ProdPad Blog, http://www.prodpad.com/blog/.

Product Focus Soapbox, http://www.productfocus.com/blog/.

Roman's Blog, http://www.romanpichler.com/blog/.

Silicon Valley Product Group Blog Articles, http://svpg.com/articles.

A Smart Bear, http://blog.asmartbear.com.

Strategic Product Manager, http://www.strategicproductmanager.com.

Succeeding with Agile—Mike Cohn's Blog, http://www.mountaingoatsoftware.com/blog.

Tyner Blain, http://tynerblain.com/blog/.

NOTES

Introduction

1. Ross F. Housholder, Molding process, US Patent US 4247508 A, filed December 3, 1979, and issued January 21, 1981.

2. For organs, see: "Engineering a Kidney," Wake Forest School of Medicine, last modified January 21, 2014, http://www.wakehealth.edu/Research/WFIRM/Research/Engineering-A-Kidney.htm.

For rockets, see: Jason Paur, "NASA Fires Up Rocket Engine Made of 3-D Printed Parts," *Wired*, August 28, 2013, http://www.wired.com/autopia/2013/08/nasa-3d-printed-rocket-engine/.

For food, see: Loura Hall, "3D Printing: Food in Space," NASA, last modified May 23, 2013, http://www.nasa.gov/directorates/spacetech/home/feature_3d_food.html.

For printers, see: RepRap, last modified October 13, 2013, http://reprap.org/.

Chapter 1: Balancing the Three Rings

1. Mind the Product is the not-for-profit umbrella organization that runs ProductTank, ProductCamp London, and the Mind the Product annual conference: Mind the Product, accessed May 5, 2014, http://www.mindtheproduct.com.

2. P&G, "A Company History: 1837–Today," last modified January 11, 2006, http://www.pg.com/translations/history_pdf/english_history.pdf.

3. An electronic copy of Neil McElroy's "brand man" memo, May 13, 1931, is archived at http://begravity.com/wp-content/uploads/2012/03/neil-mcelroy-brand-man-memo-1931.pdf (accessed May 5, 2014).

4. Ibid.

5. A production system pioneered by Toyota. "Toyota Production System," Toyota Motor Corporation, last modified March 6, 2014, http://www.toyota-global.com/company/vision_philosophy/toyota_production_system/.

6. Mark Zuckerberg, "Letter from Mark Zuckerberg," Facebook's proposed initial public offer (IPO) in its initial registration form (S-1) with the U.S. Securities and Exchange Commission, filed on February 1, 2012, p. 67, http://www.sec.gov/Archives/edgar/data/1326801/000119312512034517/d287954ds1.htm#toc287954_10.

7. Henry Blodget, "The Maturation of the Billionaire Boy-Man," *New York*, May 6, 2012, http://nymag.com/news/features/mark-zuckerberg-2012-5/index1.html.

8. "We've made a lot of mistakes building this feature, but we've made even more with how we've handled them." Mark Zuckerberg, "Thoughts on Beacon," Facebook, last modified December 5, 2007, http://www.facebook.com/notes/facebook/thoughts-on-beacon/7584397130.

9. Jay Cassano, "Secrets from Facebook's Mobile UX Testing Team," *Co.Labs*, last modified April 8, 2013, http://www.fastcolabs.com/3007979/open-company/secrets-facebooks-mobile-ux-testing-team.

10. Miniwatts Marketing Group, "Facebook Users in the World," Internet World Stats, last modified September 30, 2012, http://www.internetworldstats.com/facebook.htm.

11. Dieter Bohn, "How Facebook Secretly Redesigned Its iPhone App with Your Help," *The Verge*, September 18, 2013, http://www.theverge.com/2013/9/18/4744904/how-facebook-secretly-redesigned-its-iphone-app-with-your-help.

12. As described so neatly in Geoffrey A. Moore's must-read book, *Crossing the Chasm* (see the Further Reading list).

13. It is customary at this point to wheel out the standard hackneyed quotes about vision and motivation. The first concerns the three stonecutters ("I am building a cathedral!") from Peter F. Drucker's *The Practice of Management* (see the Further Reading list), itself lifted from a story attributed to Sir Christopher Wren. There's also its apocryphal, modern-day reinterpretation in which President John F. Kennedy asks a man cleaning the floor at NASA what he's doing ("I'm helping to send a man to the moon"). Though you've got to wonder why he had to ask in the first place—was it not obvious from the mop?

14. Dharmesh Raithatha, "Product Management, Teamwork & Company Culture at Mind Candy," speech in London at ProductTank, October 30, 2012.

15. As I observed firsthand at the inaugural Product Management Festival in Zurich, September 18, 2013, when Gabriel Steinhardt and Marty Cagan had "a bit of a falling-out" during a debate. See: Jock Busuttil, "Ich bin ein Produkt-Manager: Round-up from Inaugural Product Management Festival in Zürich," *I Manage Products* (blog), September 23, 2013, http://imanageproducts.co.uk/2013/09/23/ich-bin-ein-produkt-manager/.

16. The following short tutorials on Kaizen are instructive:

For principles, see: Steve Stephenson, "What Is Kaizen?" Graphic Products, accessed May 5, 2014, http://www.graphicproducts.com/tutorials/kaizen/.

For benefits, see: Steve Hudgik, "What Are the Benefits Resulting from Kaizen?" Graphic Products, accessed May 5, 2014, http://www.graphicproducts.com/tutorials/kaizen/kaizen-benefits.php.

17. Adrienne Tan, "6 Great Schools Around the World Where You Can Study Product Management," *Brainrants* (blog), September 27, 2012, http://www.brainmates.com.au/brainrants/6-great-schools-around-the-world-where-you-can-study-product-management. HSR Hochschule für Technik Rapperswil, Switzer-

land, has a postgraduate course specifically in software product management: MAS Software Produktmanagement, accessed May 5, 2014, http://www.hsr.ch/mas-swpm.

18. The Student-Run Computing Facility, accessed May 5, 2014, http://www.srcf.net/.

19. After moving from web server to load balancer software, Zeus Technology was acquired by Riverbed Technology in 2011. "Riverbed Expands IT Performance Business with Acquisition of Zeus Technology," Riverbed Technology, last modified July 19, 2011, http://www.riverbed.com/about/news-articles/press-releases/riverbed-expands-it-performance-business-with-acquisition-of-zeus-technology.html.

20. Primarily on the basis of its performance in the industry benchmark SPEC web99 (retired in October 2005), accessed May 5, 2014, http://www.spec.org/web99/. For example, see: John Buscemi, "IBM eServer Breaks Internet Speed Record," IBM Media Relations, http://www-03.ibm.com/press/us/en/pressrelease/1159.wss.

21. "Zeus Power 20 Million eBay Searches a Day," [*sic*] Zeus Technology, last modified June 15, 2001, archived at Internet Archive, http://web.archive.org/web/20041013162138/http://www.zeus.com/library/case_studies/ebay.pdf (accessed May 5, 2014).

22. For a comprehensive guide to running a win-loss interview, see: Sue Duris, "Win/Loss Analysis Checklist for Product Managers," *Pragmatic Marketing*, accessed May 5, 2014, http://www.pragmaticmarketing.com/resources/winloss-analysis-checklist-for-product-managers.

Chapter 2: Knowing the Customers Better Than They Know Themselves

1. Dean Kamen, Personal mobility vehicles and methods, US Patent US 6651766 B2, filed May 22, 2001, and issued November 25, 2003.

2. Rupert Goodwins, "Ginger Launch Takes Hype Biscuit," *ZDNet*, December 4, 2001, http://www.zdnet.com/ginger-launch-takes-hype-biscuit-3002100309/.

3. Steve Kemper, *Reinventing the Wheel: A Story of Genius, Innovation, and Grand Ambition*, p. 4. See the Further Reading list.

4. Ibid.

5. Marc Andreessen, "The Pmarca Guide to Startups, Part 4: The Only Thing That Matters," Pmarchive, last modified June 25, 2007, http://pmarchive.com/guide_to_startups_part4.html.

6. John Heilemann, "Reinventing the Wheel," *Time*, December 2, 2001, http://content.time.com/time/business/article/0,8599,186660-1,00.html.

7. Gary Rivlin, "Segway's Breakdown," *Wired*, March 2003, accessed May 5, 2014, http://archive.wired.com/wired/archive/11.03/segway.html. "Doerr's firm [Kleiner Perkins Caufield & Byers], it was widely reported, invested $38 million in Kamen's startup, the largest single investment in Kleiner Perkins' history. All told, Kamen raised around $90 million in the spring of 2000 in exchange for a

reported 15 percent stake in his company, which would give Segway LLC a preposterous paper worth of roughly $650 million."

8. Ibid. p. 4.

9. Martin Beckford, "Segways Banned from Pavements and Roads as Rider Fined £75," *The Telegraph*, January 19, 2011, http://www.telegraph.co.uk/finance/newsbysector/transport/8267312/Segways-banned-from-pavements-and-roads-as-rider-fined-75.html.

10. For an account of their meeting, see: Kemper, *Reinventing the Wheel*.

11. 99.999999 percent of the speed of light. See: LHC Machine Outreach, last modified July 9 2012, http://lhc-machine-outreach.web.cern.ch/lhc-machine-outreach/.

12. Or like two Nimitz-class aircraft carriers colliding at 5.6 knots: "Beam," LHC Machine Outreach, accessed May 5, 2014, http://lhc-machine-outreach.web.cern.ch/lhc-machine-outreach/beam.htm.

13. "Large Hadron Collider 'Mostly Repaired,'" *The Telegraph*, May 3, 2009, http://www.telegraph.co.uk/science/large-hadron-collider/5266415/Large-Hadron-Collider-mostly-repaired.html.

14. Before Autonomy was itself sold to HP. Robin Wauters, "Autonomy Buys Iron Mountain's Digital Archiving, Online Backup Business for $380M," *TechCrunch*, May 16, 2011, http://techcrunch.com/2011/05/16/autonomy-buys-iron-mountain%E2%80%99s-digital-archiving-online-backup-business-for-380m/.

15. Daniel Shefer provides a comprehensive guide to traditional pricing strategies in "Product and Pricing Strategies" on *Pragmatic Marketing*'s blog at http://www.pragmaticmarketing.com/resources/product-and-pricing-strategies?p=0. In the article he touches on different approaches depending on the stage within the technology adoption lifecycle, a topic also considered by Geoffrey Moore in *Crossing the Chasm* (see the Further Reading list).

Neil Davidson's book *Don't Just Roll the Dice* provides a concise overview of pricing strategy, perception of value, and fairness (see the Further Reading section).

Stewart Rogers discusses how your pricing strategy is linked to your product strategy, which is itself linked to your company's overall strategy, and so must support your company's mission. Stewart Rogers, "Pricing Strategy, Worthy of a Thought?," *Strategic Product Manager*, February 6, 2009, http://www.strategicproductmanager.com/2009/02/06/pricing-strategy-worthy-of-a-thought/.

A briefing on the Institute of Directors' website (http://www.iod.com/guidance/briefings/su-pricing-your-product-or-service) offers concise advice and questions to get you thinking about which pricing strategy to adopt. "Pricing Your Product or Service for Start-Ups," Atom Content Marketing Ltd, last modified August 7, 2013, http://www.iod.com/~/media/Documents/PDFs/IAS/BHP%20Director%20Briefings/SuB5%20Pricing%20your%20product%20or%20service.pdf.

Moving to the newer pricing strategies favored by startups, Jason Cohen covers the pros and cons of the popular freemium approach on his blog, *A Smart Bear*. You can find many other insightful articles on startup pricing strategies peppered throughout. Jason Cohen, "Reframing the Problems with 'Freemium' by Charging the Marketing Department," *A Smart Bear*, April 16, 2013, http://blog.asmartbear.com/freemium.html.

Pricing doesn't have to be based on guesswork, and A/B testing can be an effective approach to determine what the right price point should be. For a good case study of how usability testing company Clicktale evolved the pricing strategy for its software-as-a-service product through use of pricing experiments, see: Paras Chopra, "How Pricing Plans Evolved Over Time for a SaaS Startup," *I ♥ Split Testing Blog*, April 26, 2010, http://visualwebsiteoptimizer.com/split-testing-blog/how-pricing-plans-evolved-over-time-for-a-saas-startup/.

Neuromarketing is a discipline that uses consumer psychology to determine the best pricing approach. Anchor pricing is one such technique examined by Roger Dooley, "Anchor Pricing Strategies," July 18, 2008, *Neuromarketing*, http://www.neurosciencemarketing.com/blog/articles/anchor-prices.htm. Other neuromarketing pricing strategies are covered well by Stephen Forman in his two-part blog post: Stephen Forman, "Neuromarketing: Five Cutting Edge Pricing Strategies," *ProducersWEB*, February 14, 2013, http://www.producersweb.com/r/pwebmc/d/contentFocus/?pcID=fead9a4c982d05efee3b01f06f76c281, and "Neuromarketing, Pt 2: Even More Top Pricing Strategies," *ProducersWEB*, March 1, 2013, http://www.producersweb.com/r/pwebmc/d/contentFocus/?pcID=ab235cadba6bd80f411521752bcb35c6.

Lastly, behavioral economist Dan Ariely's book *Predictably Irrational* looks at how irrationality in our decision-making affects our perception of price (see the Further Reading section).

16. Joel Spolsky, cofounder of Fog Creek Software, described how his company created Trello as a free tool because their objective was to get to 100 million users as quickly as possible and then figure out how to monetize the 1 percent with premium features: Joel Spolsky, "How Trello is Different," *Joel on Software*, January 6, 2012, http://www.joelonsoftware.com/items/2012/01/06.html, and Joel Spolsky, "Free as in Fortune Cookies," *Joel on Software*, April 30, 2013, http://www.joelonsoftware.com/items/2013/04/30.html. Trello is undeniably popular, but it will be interesting to look back in a few years to see how well the freemium approach works out for them.

17. Sean Fallon, "Rong Zun 758 Razor Cellphone Features a Built-In Shaver," *Gizmodo*, April 16, 2009, http://gizmodo.com/5214890/rong-zun-758-razor-cellphone-features-a-built-in-shaver.

18. Tom Chi, "Rapid Prototyping at Google X," speech in London at Mind the Product Conference, September 28, 2012. Video: http://www.mindtheproduct.com/2012/12/rapid-prototyping-google-glass-by-tom-chi/, and slides at: http://www.slideshare.net/mindtheproduct/tom-chi-rapid-prototyping-at-google-x-mindtheproduct-2012.

19. Mark Milian, "Rejected by VCs, Pebble Watch Raises $3.8M on Kickstarter," *Bloomberg Tech Deals*, April 17, 2012, http://go.bloomberg.com/tech-deals/2012-04-17-rejected-by-vcs-pebble-watch-raises-3-8m-on-kickstarter/.

20. Pebble Technology, "Pebble: E-Paper Watch for iPhone and Android," Kickstarter, http://www.kickstarter.com/projects/597507018/pebble-e-paper-watch-for-iphone-and-android.

21. Dennis Lloyd, "Key Milestones in the Life of the iPod," *iLounge*, June 26, 2004, http://www.ilounge.com/index.php/articles/comments/instant-expert-a-brief-history-of-ipod/.

22. Bryan Chaffin, "Casady & Greene Discontinues SoundJam MP at Developer's Request," *Mac Observer*, May 6, 2001, http://www.macobserver.com/tmo/article/Casady_Greene_Discontinues_SoundJam_MP_At_Developers_Request, and Nick dePlume, "WSJ: Casady & Greene 'Forbidden' from Discussing iTunes Deal," *ThinkSecret*, July 3, 2003, archived from the original on January 16, 2008, at http://web.archive.org/web/20080116094212/http://www.thinksecret.com/news/wsjcasadygreene.html.

23. Leander Kahney, "Inside Look at Birth of the iPod," *Wired*, July 21, 2004, http://www.wired.com/gadgets/mac/news/2004/07/64286.

24. Lloyd, "Key Milestones."

25. The whole product is the core product, in this case the iPod, enhanced and made more compelling for the mass market through complementary accessories, services, and software such as iPod charging docks and the iTunes Store. The concept of "whole product" is explained in much greater detail in Moore, *Crossing the Chasm*. See the Further Reading section.

26. Powderroom, accessed May 5, 2014, http://www.powderroom.net.

27. With the 2012 Olympics, "the BBC delivered its most successful online event ever, attracting a record-breaking 55m global browsers to BBC Sport online (cumulative reach) throughout the course of the Games, and marking London 2012 as the first truly digital Games." "BBC Sport breaks online records with first truly digital Olympics," August 13, 2012, last modified March 18, 2014, BBC Media Centre, http://www.bbc.co.uk/mediacentre/latestnews/2012/sport-online-figures.html.

28. Steve Portigal, "Persona Non Grata," originally published in *Interactions*, January/February 2008, http://www.portigal.com/wp-content/uploads/2008/01/Portigal-Consulting-White-Paper-Persona-Non-Grata.pdf.

29. George Santayana, *The Life of Reason*, vol. 1, chapter XII. Available in full via Project Gutenberg at http://www.gutenberg.org/files/15000/15000-h/vol1.html.

30. Iain Thomson, "FREEZE, GLASSHOLE! California Cops Bust Google Glass Driver," *The Register*, October 30, 2013, http://www.theregister.co.uk/2013/10/30/california_cops_ticket_driver_for_wearing_google_glass/. Although Cecilia Abadie's case was dropped, this was only because there was insufficient evidence that Glass was turned on at the time: "Google Glass driver Abadie has case dropped," *BBC News*, January 17, 2014, http://www.bbc.co.uk/news/world-us-canada-25764674.

Chapter 3: You're Actually Managing People, Not Products

1. According to Matthew Glotzbach, MD, of YouTube EMEA, speaking in Zurich at Product Management Festival, September 19, 2013.

2. Aziz Musa, "Delivering a Pure Product," speech in London at the Mind the Product Conference, September 27, 2013. Video: http://www.mindtheproduct .com/2013/12/video-delivering-a-pure-product/, and slides: http://www.slideshare .net/PuristProductManagement/mind-the-product-mtpcon-aziz-musa-pure-products.

3. William Shakespeare, *The Tempest*, 3.1.64.

4. Wally Olins, "Wally Olins: Branding in Indian Companies? If Only It Were True," *Kyoorius Magazine*, November 18, 2013, http://kyoorius.com/2013/11/wally -olins-branding-in-indian-companies-if-only-it-were-true/. For more, see also the Further Reading list and Mike Atherton, "Brand-Driven Design for Content Strategy," last modified September 16, 2013, http://www.slideshare.net/reduxd/ brand-cs-forum.

5. Elon Musk, "Tesla Adds Titanium Underbody Shield and Aluminum Deflec- tor Plates to Model S," Tesla Motors, March 28, 2014, http://www.teslamotors .com/blog/tesla-adds-titanium-underbody-shield-and-aluminum-deflector-plates -model-s.

6. Gianfranco Zaccai, "Why Focus Groups Kill Innovation, from the Designer Behind Swiffer," *Co.Design*, last modified October 18, 2012, http://www.fastcodesign .com/1671033/why-focus-groups-kill-innovation-from-the-designer-behind-swiffer.

7. Tom Webster, "What's Wrong with Focus Groups?," Edison Research, December 3, 2004, http://www.edisonresearch.com/home/archives/2004/12/whats _wrong_wit.php.

8. "Handbook for New Employees," Valve Software, last modified April 17, 2012, accessed May 5, 2014, http://media.steampowered.com/apps/valve/Valve_Hand book_LowRes.pdf.

9. Thomas Jackson, Ray Dawson, and Darren Wilson, "Case Study: Evaluat- ing the Effect of Email Interruptions Within the Workplace," 2002, IN: Conference on Empirical Assessment in Software Engineering, Keele University, EASE 2002, Keele, UK, April 2002, pp. 3–7, https://dspace.lboro.ac.uk/2134/489.

10. Suw Charman-Anderson, "Breaking the Email Compulsion," *The Guard- ian*, August 28, 2008, http://www.theguardian.com/technology/2008/aug/28/email .addiction.

11. Charles Duhigg, *The Power of Habit*, p. 50. See the Further Reading section.

Chapter 4: The Fine Line Between Success and Failure

1. 1964 advertising slogan: "How to catch a salad lover with new Jell-O Salad Gelatin in vegetable flavors." "Jell-O Salad Gelatin: Celery & Mixed Vegetable Flavors (1964)," *Click Americana*, accessed May 5, 2014, http://clickamericana .com/topics/food-drink/jell-o-salad-gelatin-celery-mixed-vegetable-flavors-1964.

2. "CPSC Votes Final Ban on Lawn Darts," Consumer Product Safety Commis- sion, October 28, 1988, http://www.cpsc.gov/en/Newsroom/News-Releases/1988/ CPSC-Votes-Final-Ban-On-Lawn-Darts/.

3. The answers to the question "What is the truth behind '9 out of 10 startups fail'?" on Quora (http://www.quora.com/What-is-the-truth-behind-9-out-of-10-startups-fail)

may not provide a single, definitive statistic, but they certainly highlight the variability of factors that can contribute to the success or failure of a tech startup. Chuck Eesley's and Christoph Möller's responses to the question in particular present an array of facts and figures.

Chuck Eesley's answer: http://www.quora.com/What-is-the-truth-behind-9-out-of-10-startups-fail/answer/Chuck-Eesley.

Christoph Möller's answer: http://www.quora.com/What-is-the-truth-behind-9-out-of-10-startups-fail/answer/Christoph-M%C3%B6ller.

4. Hannah Furness, "BIC Ridiculed over Comfortable Pink Pens for Women," *The Telegraph*, August 28, 2012, http://www.telegraph.co.uk/news/newstopics/howaboutthat/9503359/BIC-ridiculed-over-comfortable-pink-pens-for-women.html.

5. Lester Haines, "Introducing Dasani—the Water with Added, er, Protein," *The Register*, March 11, 2004, http://www.theregister.co.uk/2004/03/11/introducing_dasani_the_water.

6. Bill Garrett, "Coke's Water Bomb," *BBC Money Programme*, June 16, 2004, http://news.bbc.co.uk/1/hi/business/3809539.stm.

7. In Steve Jobs's official biography. Walter Isaacson, *Steve Jobs*, p. 472. See the Further Reading section.

8. Graham Barlow and Dan Grabham, "iOS 6 Maps: What Went Wrong?," from MacFormat issue 254, *TechRadar*, December 11, 2012, http://www.techradar.com/news/software/applications/ios-6-maps-what-went-wrong-1118121.

9. "Comparing iOS 6 map image of Brooklyn Bridge," *The Amazing iOS 6 Maps* (blog), accessed May 5, 2014, http://theamazingios6maps.tumblr.com/post/32046614208/comparing-ios-6-map-image-of-brooklyn-bridge.

10. Richard Chirgwin, "Apple Maps Directs Drivers into Path of Oncoming Planes," *The Register*, September 26, 2013, http://www.theregister.co.uk/2013/09/26/apple_maps_directed_drivers_onto_alaskan_airport_taxiways/.

11. Adrian Lowe, "Tourists Stranded in Searing Heat as Apple Maps Fails," *The Sydney Morning Herald*, December 10, 2012, http://www.smh.com.au/technology/technology-news/tourists-stranded-in-searing-heat-as-apple-maps-fails-20121210-2b4n8.html.

12. Diana Huggins, "Top 10 Windows Vista Annoyances," *TechRepublic*, March 27, 2007, http://www.techrepublic.com/article/top-10-windows-vista-annoyances/.

13. Dwight Silverman, "Here's Why Your HP Printer Still Doesn't Have Vista Drivers," *Chron*, April 24, 2007, http://blog.chron.com/techblog/2007/04/heres-why-your-hp-printer-still-doesnt-have-vista-drivers/.

14. Aaron Ricadela, "Closing the Door to Microsoft Vista," *Bloomberg Businessweek*, May 13, 2008, http://www.businessweek.com/stories/2008-05-13/closing-the-door-to-microsoft-vistabusinessweek-business-news-stock-market-and-financial-advice.

15. "Thirteen years after it was released, Windows XP remains the world's second most popular PC operating system. It's running on 27.69 per cent of consumer machines, according to market stats from beancounters Netcraft." Gavin

Clarke, "Windows XP is Finally Dead, Right? Er, Not Quite. Here's What to Do If You're Stuck with It," *The Register*, April 8, 2014, http://www.theregister.co.uk/2014/04/08/end_of_xp/.

16. The Royal Bank of Scotland suffered a massive outage for a few days in July 2012 due to a failed systems upgrade. While the defective software component that caused the problem was identified, in the view of analysts and a former RBS employee, rectifying the fault took far longer than it should have due to the inherent bureaucracy of the change management process. Anna Leach, "RBS Must Realize It's Just an IT Biz with a Banking Licence," *The Register*, August 1, 2012, http://www.theregister.co.uk/2012/08/01/how_can_banks_stop_it_crashes_happening_again/.

17. For a basic introduction to APIs, see the Wikipedia page at http://en.wikipedia.org/wiki/Application_programming_interface.

18. Ken Schwaber and Jeff Sutherland, *The Scrum Guide™—The Definitive Guide to Scrum: The Rules of the Game*, Scrum.org, October 2011, https://www.scrum.org/Portals/0/Documents/Scrum Guides/2013/Scrum-Guide.pdf.

19. Roman Pichler, "What Is Agile Product Management?," *Roman's Blog*, March 1, 2010, http://www.romanpichler.com/blog/what-is-agile-product-management/.

20. If you want to take a more statistically minded approach, there's a helpful online velocity calculator at http://www.mountaingoatsoftware.com/tools/velocity-range-calculator.

21. The Business Model Canvas is designed by Business Model Foundry AG, the makers of Business Model Generation and Strategyzer (http://www.businessmodelgeneration.com/). This work is licensed under the Creative Commons Attribution-ShareAlike 3.0 Unported License. To view a copy of this license, visit: http://creativecommons.org/licenses/by-sa/3.0/. You can find it as an interactive tool online. The official apps can be found at http://www.businessmodelgeneration.com/toolbox or a good, free alternative is at http://canvanizer.com/.

22. Janna Bastow, "Tame Your Roadmap," *Mind the Product* (blog), September 27, 2011, http://www.mindtheproduct.com/2011/09/tame-your-roadmap/.

23. Simon Cast, "Roadmapping Without Dates," *ProdPad* (blog), January 24, 2013, http://www.prodpad.com/2013/01/roadmapping-without-dates/.

24. You can see ProdPad's current public roadmap at http://www.prodpad.com/our-roadmap/.

25. FreeAgent's roadmap is at: http://depot.freeagent.com/. It is far more chirpy than you'd expect for a company providing online bookkeeping software.

26. Cory Bennett and Ariel Tseitlin, "Chaos Monkey Released into the Wild," *The Netflix Tech Blog*, July 30, 2012, http://techblog.netflix.com/2012/07/chaos-monkey-released-into-wild.html.

27. Duhigg, *The Power of Habit*, 103–104. See the Further Reading section.

28. For a masterful article on why the saying is nonsense, see: Victor H. Mair, professor of Chinese language and literature at the University of Pennsylvania,

"Danger + Opportunity ≠ Crisis," Pinyin Info, last modified September 2009, http://www.pinyin.info/chinese/crisis.html.

29. Douglas MacMillan, "Andreessen: This Isn't a Tech Bubble," *Wall Street Journal*, January 5, 2014, http://online.wsj.com/news/articles/SB40001424052702303640604579298330921690014.

30. Chi, "Rapid Prototyping at Google X."

Chapter 5: Tender Loving Care of Time

1. Peter F. Drucker, *The Effective Executive*, p. 26. See the Further Reading section.

2. Marty Cagan, "Product Manager vs. Product Owner," *Silicon Valley Product Group* (blog), December 6, 2011, http://svpg.com/product-manager-vs-product-owner/.

3. Frank Partnoy, *Wait: The Art and Science of Delay*. See the Further Reading section.

4. C. Northcote Parkinson, "Parkinson's Law," *The Economist*, November 19, 1955, archived at http://www.economist.com/node/14116121 (accessed May 5, 2014).

5. Stuart Dreyfus, "System 0: The Overlooked Explanation of Expert Intuition" (forthcoming), last modified May 25, 2013, http://www.ieor.berkeley.edu/People/Faculty/dreyfus-pubs/Expert_Intuition.pdf.

6. Kahneman, *Thinking, Fast and Slow*, p. 12. See the Further Reading list.

7. Sylvain Charron and Etienne Koechlin, "Divided Representation of Concurrent Goals in the Human Frontal Lobes," *Science*, April 16, 2010, http://www.sciencemag.org/content/328/5976/360.short.

8. Issie Lapowsky, "Don't Multitask: Your Brain Will Thank You," *Inc.*, April 17, 2013, http://www.inc.com/magazine/201304/issie-lapowsky/get-more-done-dont-multitask.html.

9. "The Siren Song of Multitasking," Herman Miller, last modified January 15, 2007, http://www.hermanmiller.com/content/dam/hermanmiller/documents/research_summaries/wp_SirenSong.pdf.

10. Martin Hilbert and Priscilla López, "The World's Technological Capacity to Store, Communicate, and Compute Information," *Science*, April 1, 2011, http://www.sciencemag.org/content/332/6025/60.

11. John M. Grohol, "FOMO Addiction: The Fear of Missing Out," *PsychCentral* (blog), April 14, 2011, http://psychcentral.com/blog/archives/2011/04/14/fomo-addiction-the-fear-of-missing-out/.

Conclusion

1. "'Twerking' and 'Selfie' Added to Oxford Dictionary," *BBC News*, August 28, 2013, http://www.bbc.co.uk/news/entertainment-arts-23861702.

INDEX

Page numbers of illustrations appear in *italics*.

Adams, Douglas, 139
Agile product development, 122-24, 131
Amazon, 32
Andreessen, Marc, 33, 57, 136-37
Apple, 1, 147
  iPhone, 60, 76, 113-14, *114*, 118
  iPod and iTunes, *56*, 56-57, 110
  Maps, ix-x, 2, 107-8
application programming interface,
    117-18

Bastow, Janna, 129, 130, 174
Bennett, Cory, 134
best practices, 106-38
  agile development, 122-24
  assessing upgrades appeal, 115-18
  avoiding epic failures, 133-34
  building three business cases, 110,
    111, 138
  end-of-life for products, 117, 118-20, *120*
  good communication, 112-13, 138
  knowing how to respond to a crisis,
    134-38
  learning from successes, 113-15
  right timing of market entry, 108-9
  seeking out lightbulb moments, 126-28
  solving "second album problem,"
    120-21
  sticking to area of expertise,
    109-10, 138

using a product roadmap, 128-32
warning others about changes,
    132-33
whole product must be ready, 106-8
Bezos, Jeff, 36-37
Blackblot, 25
Blanchard, Ken, 93-94
brand/branding, 80, 104
Brand Failures (Haig), 103n
Branson, Sir Richard, 50
Bush, George W., 33, *34*
business
  common errors, 69, 97
  flat organization structure, 89
  three rings and, 8-9, 168
business case, 110, *111*, 127, 138
Business Model Canvas, 127, *127*

Cagan, Marty, 140-41
Cast, Simon, 129, 130, 174-75
Chi, Tom, 52, 53, 127
Coca-Cola
  Dasani water, 105, 112
  New Coke, 103, 104-5
cognitive ease, 91
communication, 97-100, 102, 138
  emails, 97-99, 152, 156, *157*
  product failure and poor, 112-13
  stopping distractions of, 154-57, 162
Continuum design group, 82

crisis management, 134–37, 138
Crossing the Chasm (Moore), 55, 106
cruft, 119
customers, 29–67
  early adopters or "earlyvangelists," 55
  how to delight (feature choice), 57–60
  Kano model for satisfaction, 57–60
  latent needs, 59, 65, 67
  motivation to buy, 41–45, 67
  needs of, 30, 33–36, 38–39, 45–46, 55, 67
  PM and, 30, 46, 55, 60–65, 67
  product features vs. benefits and,
    46–49, 67
  product upgrades and, 115–18
  product value and, 44–45, 67
  roadmap for, 132
  user personas, 62–64, 67

data analytics, 11–13, 28, 84, 115
designers, 75–79, 102
development team (engineering), 9,
    70–75, 102
  measuring velocity of, 124
Doerr, John, 31–32, 33, 34–35, 36
Drucker, Peter, 139
Duhigg, Charles, 98, 135

eBay, 19
Effective Executive, The (Drucker), 139
Eriksson, Martin, 6, 7, 8
Experian, 91–92, 171–72

Facebook, 12, 37, 109
focus groups, 81–83
Ford Edsel, 103, 103n
FreeAgent, 86, 132
Frito-Lay Lemonade, ix, 104, 109

Gladwell, Malcolm, 149
Google, 1, 15, 133–34, 176
  Glass, 52–53, 54, 66–67, 66n, 105, 137–38
  Maps, 107
Grohol, John, 152

Haig, Matt, 103n
Hersey, Paul, 93–94
Hilbert, Martin, 152
  horizon planning, 124
Housholder, Ross F., 1

Innocent Drinks, *59*, 59
Inspired (Cagan), 140
Iron Mountain, 43–44, 110, 168–69

Jobs, Steve, 31, 57, 107
Johnson, Steve, 25

Kahneman, Daniel, 91, 148
kaizen (continual improvement), 16
Kamen, Dean, 31–33, 35, 36
Kano model, 57–60, *58*, 84, 109
Kemper, Steve, 31, 32, 33
Kickstarter, 53
Knox safety armor, *47*, 47–48

lacunae, 65
Large Hadron Collider, CERN, 1,
    40–41, 40n
Larsen, Norm, 55
*Leadership and the One Minute
    Manager* (Blanchard et al), 93n
Lean Manufacturing, 11–12
Lean Startup, The (Ries), 50, 54
Lean Startup theory, 1, 133, 136
Levenstein, Aaron, 13
Levitt, Theodore, 84
Life Savers soda, 104, 109
lightbulb moments, 126–28

MailChimp, 86
market gaps, 38, *39*, 67
market opportunity, 15
marketing team, 79–86, 102
Maslow, Abraham, 1, 45, 48
Mayer, Marissa, 176
Maylon, Paul, 173
McElroy, Neil, 10, 11

McLean, Lucie, 62, 63–64, 148
Microsoft, 110
  Surface/Surface 2, 109
  Windows versions, 116, 119
Miller, Luke, 62
Mind Candy, 15
minimum viable products (MVPs), 1,
    50–57, *54*, *56*, 108
  concierge, 53
  Ries's cyclical approach, 50, 51
  when to make, 55–57
Moore, Geoffrey, 55
MoSCoW method, 73–74
Musa, Aziz, 76

NASA, 135
Nass, Clifford, 150–51
Netflix, 3
  Chaos Monkey, 134
Netscape, 32, 33
No Exit (Sartre), 69
Nokia, 110

Olins, Wally, 80
Oppenheimer, Danny, 91
organizational dysfunctions, 69, 70,
    81–82
Outliers (Gladwell), 149

Palm Pilot, 76
Parkinson's Law, 144
Partnoy, Frank, 144
Pebble watch, 53–54, *54*
Pichler, Roman, 122
pivots, 54–55
Portigal, Steve, 64
Powderroom, 62
Power of Habit, The (Duhigg), 98, 135
*Practitioner's Guide to User Experience
    Design, The* (Miller), 62
Pragmatic Marketing, 25
pricing, 43–45
procrastination, 3, 159–61, 162

Procter & Gamble (P&G), 10
ProdPad, 130–31
product development, 9, 11
  agile development, 122–24
  assumptions and, 35, 36, 37, 49–57,
    67, 132
  customer/market analysis, 31, 35,
    38–49, *39*
  data and real-time analytics, 11–12
  feature choices, 57–60
  features vs. benefits, 46–49, 100
  flawed business plans, 35
  methodologies for, 1–12
  MVPs and, 50–57, *54*, *56*, 67
  pivots, 54–55
  product pricing, 43–45
  risk and, 37, 38–39
  "second album problem," 120
  Segway example, 31–36
product failure, 103–13, 115, 135. *See
    also* Segway; *specific products*
  causes, 104–21
  classic, ix, 31–36, 103–4, 103n
  crisis management and, 134–37
  "failing fast," 133, 136, 137
Product Focus, 25
product launches, 1, 6, 105, 112,
    113–14, *114*
  right timing of market entry, 108–9
  whole product must be ready, 106–8
product management team, 3, 68–102.
    See also specific members
  corporate higher-ups and, 89–92
  PM leadership of, approaches, 92–97
  stakeholder map for, 95–97
product manager (PM), ix, 1, 6
  activities competing for attention,
    125, *125*
  author's Golden Rule, 69
  author's route to, including RAF
    training, 5, *18*, 18–21, *21*, 25, 146–47,
    168–69, 171–72
  best practices, 106–38

product manager (PM) (*cont.*)
career routes to, 17–18, 22, 167–75
"CEO of the product" mislabel, 69
communication and, 97–100
competing approaches to role of, 15–18, 25
courses and training for, 16–17, 25
customers and, 30, 46, 55, 60–65, 67
flexibility of approach and, 26, 106
hiring offers, considerations, 26–27
job description, 6–7
job qualifications, 15, 22
learning the basics, 24–25
managing down and up, 89–97
McLean as, 63–64
ownership and vision, 13–16, 22–23, 28
as people manager, 68–102
performance indicators for, 163–65
questions to ask yourself, 26–27
risk reduction and, 37, 38–39
role of, primary, 100
roots of profession, 10
saying no, 100–101, 102
skills needed, ix, 3, 13, 17, 27, 140
three rings of, 7–10, 27, 69–70
time management and, 139–62
traits of, 22–24, 23n, 101–2
as "the voice of the customer," 65, 67
wrong reasons for career choice, 165–67
product roadmap, 128–32, *130*, *131*
product vision, 6, 9, 13–15, 16, 28, 33, 65, 69, 71, 102, 104, 123, 128
"pure products," 76

Raithatha, Dharmesh, 15
Reebok Pump, 1, 82
Reinventing the Wheel (Kemper), 32
Ries, Eric, 50, 55, 133, 137
risk, 37, 65–66, 67, 135
testing assumptions and, 49–57
Rong Zun 758 Razor mobile phone, 49
Rwanda testing bias, 2, 82, 172

sales team, 86–89, 102
Santayana, George, 66
Sartre, Jean-Paul, 69
Schmidt, Eric, 107
Schwaber, Ken, 122
Scrum, 122–23, 160–61
Scrum Guide (Schwaber and Sutherland), 122
Segway, ix, 31–36, 50, 104, 105, 113
Sequent Learning Network, 25
Shakespeare, William, 76
Silicon Valley Product Group, 25
situational leadership, 3, 93–95, 93n
Socrates, 31, 35
Sony, 103
South Park "Gnomes" episode, 35
Stafford, Tom, 97
stakeholder map, 95–97, *96*
startups, 19, 33, 41, 42–43
PM in, 16, 38, 169
"second album problem," 120–21
success, 34n, 163–65, 175–76
examples of specific PMs, 173–75
Sutherland, Jeff, 122

target market, 6, 8, 10, 25, 36, 39–40, 60–64, 67, 79
technology, 1, 6, 9, 10–11, 17, 22, 25, 30, 31, 31n, 35, 39, 133, 137, 141, 176
three rings and, 8, 9, 10, 168
Tempest, The (Shakespeare), 76
Tesla Motors, 80
Thinking, Fast and Slow (Kahneman), 91, 148
3-D printers, 1
three rings, 7, 7–10, 22, 168
achieving balance, 9–12, 27–28
PM at center of, 8, 69
time management, 139–62, *143*
Toohey, Brian, 36
Trello, 48–49
Tseitlin, Ariel, 134

user personas, 62–64, *63*, *64*, 67
UX (user experience), 8, 17, 62, 168
  designers, 77–78

Valve software company, 89
Viagra (sildenafil citrate), 13
Virgin Atlantic, 50–51, 54

Wait (Partnoy), 144
Waterfall serial project development
  process, 11, 73

WD-40, 55
Webster, Tom, 83
Wenger Giant Swiss Army
    Knife, 60
win-loss interviews, 20–21

Zaccai, Gianfranco, 82
Zeno, 145
Zeus Technology, 16, 19–20, 72–73,
    81, 92
Zuckerberg, Mark, 12

ABOUT THE AUTHOR

Jock Busuttil is a product consultant, speaker, and writer. He has spent more than a decade working as a product manager for technology companies ranging in size from startups to multinationals, including Zeus Technology, Iron Mountain, and Experian. In 2012, he founded Product People (productpeo.pl), a product management consultancy. With a number of associates, he provides help to companies large and small needing an extra pair of hands, and his clients include After the  Flood, BBC, eWise, Inkling, SwiftServe, and What Users Do.

Jock routinely teaches classes at General Assembly on product management and mentors startups, entrepreneurs, and product professionals. He holds a master's degree in classics from the University of Cambridge, UK; is the author of the blog *I Manage Products* (imanageproducts.co.uk); and regularly contributes articles to *Mind the Product* (mindtheproduct.com). You can tweet him @jockbu and can generally find him at ProductTank each month in London.